Cambridge Elements ≡

Elements in Child Development
edited by
Marc H. Bornstein
*National Institute of Child Health and Human Development,
Bethesda Institute for Fiscal Studies, London
UNICEF, New York City*

CHILDREN'S DEFENSIVE MINDSET

Kenneth A. Dodge
*Duke University – Sanford School of Public Policy
Durham*

CAMBRIDGE
UNIVERSITY PRESS

CAMBRIDGE
UNIVERSITY PRESS

Shaftesbury Road, Cambridge CB2 8EA, United Kingdom

One Liberty Plaza, 20th Floor, New York, NY 10006, USA

477 Williamstown Road, Port Melbourne, VIC 3207, Australia

314–321, 3rd Floor, Plot 3, Splendor Forum, Jasola District Centre, New Delhi – 110025, India

103 Penang Road, #05–06/07, Visioncrest Commercial, Singapore 238467

Cambridge University Press is part of Cambridge University Press & Assessment, a department of the University of Cambridge.

We share the University's mission to contribute to society through the pursuit of education, learning and research at the highest international levels of excellence.

www.cambridge.org
Information on this title: www.cambridge.org/9781009509831

DOI: 10.1017/9781009416207

First published 2024

A catalogue record for this publication is available from the British Library.

ISBN 978-1-009-50983-1 Hardback
ISBN 978-1-009-41623-8 Paperback
ISSN 2632-9948 (online)
ISSN 2632-993X (print)

Children's Defensive Mindset

Elements in Child Development

DOI: 10.1017/9781009416207
First published online: May 2024

Kenneth A. Dodge
Duke University – Sanford School of Public Policy Durham

Author for correspondence: Kenneth A. Dodge, dodge@duke.edu

Abstract: The primary psychological process leading aggressive children to grow into dysfunctional adults is a defensive mindset, which encompasses a pattern of deviant social information processing steps, including hypervigilance to threat; hostile attributional biases; psychophysiological reactivity, experience of rage and testosterone release (in males); aggressive problem-solving styles; aggressogenic decision-making biases; and deficient behavioral skills. These processes are acquired in childhood and predict adult maladjustment outcomes, including incarceration and premature death. The antecedents of defensive mindset lie in early childhood experiences of trauma and threat. The Fast Track (FT) intervention was designed to improve social competence in aggressive children. A randomized controlled trial demonstrated that FT is effective in preventing externalizing psychopathology; the primary mediating factor is the reduction of defensive mindset processes. This Element concludes with insights that defensive mindset might also explain dysfunction in other realms, including school culture, parenting, marriage, the workplace, intergroup relationships, politics, and international relations.

This element also has a video abstract: www.cambridge.org/EICD-Kenneth

Keywords: defensive mindset, social information processing, aggression, prevention, trauma

ISBNs: 9781009509831 (HB), 9781009416238 (PB), 9781009416207 (OC)
ISSNs: 2632-9948 (online), 2632-993X (print)

Contents

1 Introduction

Rocky was a 12-year-old inpatient at an adolescent psychiatric hospital in the 1970s. One day, following a disruption on the ward, his psychotherapist approached him from behind, tapping him on the shoulder to say hello. In a nanosecond, Rocky turned around, clenched his fist, and punched the therapist hard in the gut. A second later, Rocky recognized his therapist, whom he liked, and pulled back his fist, saying, "Aw, geez, I didn't know it was you. You can't be too careful around here." Rocky's behavior reflects a pattern called *defensive mindset*. This Element is about a lifetime of research to understand and reduce the defensive mindset.

Defensive mindset is an acquired way of approaching the social world. The person with a defensive mindset is always on alert, hypervigilant, and ready to detect and respond to threats. Even ambiguous cues by another person (e.g., an awkward half-smile that might be a cynical taunt, laughing after someone falls to the ground, or a tap on the shoulder) quickly get encoded as threat. The defensive-minded person is perceptually ready to interpret these ambiguous provocation cues as hostile and to experience emotions of fear and anxiety. The person's heart immediately races, palms sweat, testosterone is released, neural pathways in the amygdala brain region activate, and the whole body mobilizes into defensive mode with a singular goal of self-preservation. Think "code red," blood flooding the brain, and emergency horns blaring. The defensive mindset triggers behavioral responses such as hitting back and screaming, designed to mitigate the perceived threat. Long-term consequences be damned, the person must survive the immediate onslaught. The person responds by acting now and thinking later.

Not all social interactions go this way for the defensive-minded person. Trust is still possible, but only with a treasured few and perhaps only after a long trial period. And not all defensive-minded persons have impulsively severe reactions – this is a dimensional characteristic. We all might have a little defensive mindedness in us, and it might come out only under rare but specific circumstances, or perhaps it shows in only one relationship. Think of that bully in fourth grade who constantly made fun of you and always got your goat. Or think of that irritating relative who knows how to push your buttons.

One of the most vexing characteristics of the defensive mindset is that it is self-reinforcing. Once established, it is very difficult to extinguish. It becomes a self-fulfilling prophecy. No amount of "talk therapy" was able to convince Rocky otherwise; his own experiences led him to a defensive mindset, his own experiences reinforced that mindset every day, and only a long repetition of new counter-experiences might (maybe, we hope) change the defensive mindset.

A prominent hypothesis in the 1970s (Selman, 1976) was that chronically aggressive children have a deficit in a specific social-cognitive skill that Piaget called spatial role-taking. Perhaps these children are unable to "see" things from someone else's perspective. Piaget conducted experiments in which a young focal child was seated in a room facing a paper maché "mountain" with irregular peaks and valleys. Another child was seated on the opposite side of the mountain, and the focal child's task was to describe the visual image actually seen by the other child. Young children are quite bad at this task, but older children get the idea and become able to generate and hold in memory an image of what other people see. Perhaps if aggressive children could be taught the skill of spatial role-taking (i.e., teaching them to "see" what others see), they would more likely take the social role of peers in social interactions, interpret peers' actions more benignly, and react less aggressively.

This hypothesis led me (Dodge, 1976) as a graduate student to design an intervention for aggressive children to train them in role-taking skills and to test the impact of this intervention through a randomized controlled trial with groups of socially rejected, aggressive 12-year-old boys who were assigned to either an intervention or control condition. The role-taking training intervention used video cameras to show boys what other children "see" during actual social encounters, and the impact on boys' behavioral adjustment was tested at the end of the school year. It was a highly successful experiment in the scientific sense, showing with great scientific certainty that, to my disappointment, the role-taking intervention had absolutely no effect on improving the behavior of aggressive children (Dodge, 1976).

Before I dared to attempt another intervention experiment, I sought to understand better the mental processes that lead some children to aggress toward others. It would be 10 years before I returned to intervention. In retrospect, it became clear the analogy to Piaget's spatial role-taking phenomenon was a poor model for what aggressive children experience. Aggressive children are not indiscriminately bad at detecting others' perspectives. In fact, they are better than most children at accurately detecting hostile intentions in others with minimal input; what is challenging for these children is accurately detecting (and believing) that others might have benign intentions.

Clinical experiences like that with Rocky (I was the therapist who was hit in the gut), coupled with 10 years of laboratory experiments, suggested that socially competent children process social information through an online sequence of mental steps. In contrast, aggressive children perform in a biased way at each of these steps and demonstrate a pattern of processing social information that includes many components: hypervigilance to threat cues, a tendency to be biased toward making hostile attributions, psychophysiological hyperreactivity to threat, exaggerated testosterone release, adoption of defensive goals, aggressive problem-solving styles, impulsive decision-making responses that favor immediate self-defense, and exquisite skill in acting out aggressive behaviors.

Colleagues and I have conducted longitudinal studies following young defensive-minded children into adulthood to discover that these children are at risk for tragic adult life outcomes, including mental health problems, chronic unemployment, violent crimes, incarceration, and even premature deaths. Looking back at children's earliest years showed that most children who acquire a defensive mindset had had early experiences of physical abuse, harsh parenting, or chronic rejection by peers. These experiences led many of them to develop a defensive mindset as a way to adapt to horrible circumstances. Although the defensiveness might have had short-term adaptive value, it also perpetuated their social problems and cascaded into more severe outcomes in adulthood.

Returning to intervention, these studies of defensive mindset, along with colleagues' studies of parenting, academic skills, and peer relationships, provided a rationale for the Conduct Problems Prevention Research Group (CPPRG, 1999) to design a multi-component intervention for aggressive children called Fast Track. A rigorous randomized controlled trial (CPPRG, 2002) demonstrated that aggressive children assigned to Fast Track fared better than those assigned as controls in measures of defensive mindset and other indicators of behavioral adjustment during childhood. Twenty years later, children assigned to the Fast Track intervention at age six enjoyed better adult outcomes than did control children in lower criminality and psychopathology and higher rates of marriage and well-being.

Section 2 of this Element describes the phenomenon of defensive mindset and recounts experiments that show how it characterizes the phenomenological and physiological experiences of children who grow into chronically aggressive behavior problems. Section 3 synthesizes these studies into a general model of social information processing that articulates the mental steps human beings follow when responding to social situations. Section 4 reports several long-term prospective studies in which samples of children were followed from early childhood into adulthood. The findings are clear and worrisome: Children who develop a defensive mindset are more likely than others to suffer violent and maladaptive outcomes in adulthood. Section 5 looks back to earlier in the lifespan to report longitudinal studies showing that adverse early life experiences, particularly child maltreatment by parents and chronic social rejection by peers, predispose some children to develop a defensive mindset, which cascades into lifelong maladaptive outcomes. Section 6 describes the Fast Track preventive intervention with six-year-old aggressive children and the impact it has on these children when they grow into adults. Section 7 provides some principles about how institutional structures might be shaped to keep children from developing a defensive mindset and provides insights that the phenomenon of defensive mindset could apply to interpersonal relationship problems in everyday life spanning marital relationships, parent–child relationships, workplace conflicts, and even international relations between nations. The Element closes by suggesting defensive mindset has played a pivotal role in global conflicts, including the Cold War and Mideast terrorism.

2 What is Defensive Mindset?

Defensive mindset can be a good thing: It has enabled the human species to survive across millennia. Evolutionary theorists have hypothesized that it is adaptive for humans to react aggressively when attacked by fellow humans. Axelrod (1981) proposed a "tit for tat" rule (defined as "retaliation in kind") that he argued evolved as an adaptive way to contain violence and promote cooperation in the species, as long as the response to provocation is neither too strong nor too weak. "Too strong" would mean overreacting to a minor provocation or reacting aggressively to ambiguous attacks or non-provocations that are interpreted as attacks. In fact, *Axelrod hypothesized that overinterpreting provocations as threats is the primary process responsible for escalation of conflict both interpersonally and between nations.* "Too weak" would mean failing to recognize and respond to a genuine threat. Axelrod's studies in political science involved presenting hypothetical scenarios of ambiguous provocation to research participants iteratively across short periods of time, and his findings became the basis for contemporary game theory.

Contemporary neuroscience offers a dynamic account of the brain as a predictive system, one in which the brain is constantly anticipating the future needs of the body before they occur, predicting future experiences to meet those needs, and updating those predictions to make more accurate predictions in the future. Sinclair et al. (2023) have identified brain regions implicated in defensive responding. They assert the amygdala prioritizes self-protection and defensive aggression during stress, whereas the hippocampus is implicated in problem solving, curiosity, learning, and exploration and enables longer-term growth and success. They called the former a "stressed mindset" and the latter a "curious mindset."

Two hypotheses stem from this work:

(1) *Within-child associations:* Given an ambiguous provocation by a peer (e.g., being touched from behind, having milk spilled on one's lap), if a child interprets the provocation as intentional and hostile, that child will react with aggressive behavior); in contrast, when that same child interprets the provocation as a non-intentional accident, that child will react nonaggressively;

and

(2) *Between-child associations:* The child who regularly attributes hostile intent to ambiguous peer provocations (called a hostile attributional bias) will develop chronic aggressive behavior problems and become maladjusted (because the hippocampus is not developing curious learning).

Hypothesis 1 is the "tit-for-tat" heuristic that Axelrod posed as being borne in evolution. It has similarities to the Old Testament concepts of "eye for an eye and tooth for a tooth," and humans tend to follow it to keep order. Hypothesis 2 is tempering: Hostile attributions too often or in too many circumstances lead to unfortunate outcomes such as chronic aggressive behavioral problems. Call this the defensive mindset problem.

2.1 Hostile Attributional Bias Is Associated with Retaliatory Aggressive Behavior

After the spatial role-taking intervention failed and observing children like Rocky, I tested the fundamental hypotheses in my doctoral dissertation with 7-to-12-year-old boys (half chronically aggressive as rated by classroom teachers and peer nominations, and half well-adjusted and nonaggressive). The studies focused on hostile attributional bias, which is one component of defensive mindedness. Boys were asked to imagine being in different social situations in which a peer engages in an ambiguous provocation act such as touching them on the shoulder from behind or spilling milk on their lap. Boys were asked to imagine being the object of the provocation and to explain the likely reason for the act, coded according to the intention the child attributed to the peer as "benign-accidental" or "hostile-intentional." Children were then asked what they would do in response to the provocation, coded as "retaliate aggressively" or not.

The findings were clear (Dodge, 1980). When children attributed a hostile intent to the peer, they had a 60% chance of saying they would retaliate aggressively, whereas when children attributed a benign intent to the peer, they had only a 26% chance of saying they would retaliate aggressively. This robust association supports the first hypothesis and suggests that most children follow Axelrod's "tit for tat" rule. The second hypothesis was also supported: the chronically aggressive group of children was 50% more likely than the non-aggressive group to make a hostile attribution about the peer provocateur (base rates of 25% versus 17%, respectively).

These findings have been replicated in over 400 studies by different research teams using a wide variety of stimuli to depict provocations with diverse samples of children. Independent meta-analyses of studies with children (Orbio de Castro et al., 2002) and adults (Tuente et al., 2019) yield robust findings of moderate-size effects that hold across ethnic groups that include non-Hispanic White, African American, and Latin American children (Graham et al., 1992). Katsurada and Sugawara (1998) observed the phenomenon in children as young as preschoolers, and Steinberg and Dodge (1983) observed it among adolescents. Feldman and Dodge (1987) replicated it across ages and genders in a school population, and Milich and Dodge (1984) identified the pattern in a child psychiatric population. Dodge et al. (1990) reported it among severely violent adolescents, and Lochman and Dodge (1994) replicated it among both violent and moderately aggressive boys. Several years ago, Verhoef et al. (2019) updated their meta-analysis with 111 new studies involving over 29,000 participants and found the relation remains robust.

The phenomenon is not unique to Western culture. A significant relation between children's hostile attributional bias and chronic aggressive behavior problems has been found in South Korea (Yoo & Park, 2019), Turkey (Aktas et al., 2005), and China (Quan et al., 2019). Lansford's Parenting Across Cultures (PAC) study with 1,299 8-year-old children from 12 diverse cultural groups around the globe has shown robust support for the two hypotheses. Across experiences within a child, when a child attributed hostile intention to a peer provocateur, that child was more likely to respond with retaliatory aggressive behavior than when that same child attributed a benign intention to the peer (Dodge et al., 2015; Figure 1). In addition, those children who displayed a pattern of hostile attributional biases were more likely to have chronic aggressive behavioral problems several years into the future. These patterns held in each of the 12 cultures.

A curious finding in the PAC study was the vast differences across cultures in the overall rate at which children made hostile attributions about their peers. In Zarqa, Jordan; Naples, Italy; and among African Americans in Durham, North Carolina, children made hostile attributions about half of the time (54%, 46%, and 48% of the time, respectively), whereas in Jinan, China; Manila,

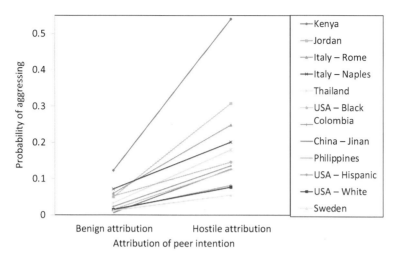

Figure 1 The tendency to react aggressively following a hostile attribution is universal: The relation between hostile attributional bias and retaliatory aggressive behavior in 12 cultures (adapted from Dodge et al., 2015).

Philippines; and Trollhättan/Vänersborg, Sweden, children made hostile attributions only about a quarter of the time (17%, 29%, and 31%, respectively). Incredibly, culture-wide rates of hostile attributional bias accounted for culture-wide rates of children's aggressive behavior problems. Thus, the PAC study supported a third hypothesis, that the cultures with the highest rates of hostile attributional bias would also have the highest rates of aggressive behavior problems (Dodge et al., 2015).

Could it be that some cultures foster hostile attributional bias in their children to a greater degree than do other cultures? Nisbett (1996) described the US South historically as a "culture of honor" in which parents, institutions, and leaders actively encourage children to take umbrage at being "dishonored" and to defend themselves at every opportunity. Anderson (1989) described a "code of the street" in American inner cities in which being "dissed" (as in disrespected) triggers a requirement to retaliate. Lansford and Dodge (2008) speculated that perhaps something in a culture's ecology, economy, or past experiences predisposes that culture to socialize their children to become defensive-minded, and differences in defensive mindset across cultures are a partial reason for cultural differences in the population-wide rates that children engage in aggressive behavior. To test this hypothesis, they scoured the Standard Cross-cultural Sample of anthropological records from 186 diverse cultures around the world and across time. Coders rated ethnographic records on a scale of 0 to 9 for the degree to which children were socialized to use defensive aggression through a process called "inculcation" that included corporal punishment for not defending oneself and admonitions to stand up for oneself. Independent coders scored the overall level of aggressive behavior among children, and still other coders scored the extent to which a culture had past experience with external warfare. Lansford and Dodge discovered that those cultures that inculcated their children toward defensiveness had higher rates of aggressive behavior among their children and adults. Moreover, those cultures that had previously experienced the most cross-nation warfare were most likely to inculcate children in this way. Societal experiences of war, threat, and danger may lead parents to socialize their children to become defensive minded, which protects children from imminent international threat but leads children to engage in high rates of aggressive behavior toward peers.

2.2 Hostile Attributional Bias Leads to Growth in Aggressive Behavior Problems

Which comes first, a hostile attributional bias or chronic aggressive behavior problems? It is plausible that some children develop chronic aggressive behavior problems first, then experience social punishment from peers for their problematic behavior, and then observe hostile acts from peers and make hostile attributions about their peers – in that order, with no causal influence of hostile attributional biases on children's behavioral and adjustment outcomes. The correlational studies reported above are intriguing, but they must be subject to more rigorous tests about causality, including experiments and prospective studies.

In an experiment as part of my dissertation (Dodge, 1980), chronically aggressive and nonaggressive boys were brought into the laboratory one by one and exposed to real-life provocations. Each boy was asked to engage in a puzzle-making contest for a prize with an unknown peer next door. Halfway through the contest, the boys took a break. While resting in the lounge, the boy "overheard" the peer enter his room through an intercom system (actually, a pre-recorded audio message).

At this point, the boy experienced one of three randomly assigned conditions. In the hostile experimental condition, the "peer" made the following statement, in a hostile voice:

> *"Gee, it looks like he's got a lot done. Well, I don't like it. I don't want him to win that dumb prize, so there, I'll mess it up."* [Crashing sounds are heard.]

In the benign condition, the peer stated in a friendly voice:

> *"Gee it looks like he's got a lot done. I think I'll help him put some more pieces together. Hey, there's one. I'll put it here."* [Crashing sounds are heard.] *"Oh, no, hey, I didn't mean to drop it."*

In the ambiguous condition, the peer made only the following statement:

> "*Gee it looks like he's got a lot done.*" [After a pause, crashing sounds are heard.].

In all three conditions, the outcome for the boy was identical: his puzzle was destroyed by the actions of the peer and he would lose the prize. The only difference was the peer's stated intention, as hostile, benign, or ambiguous. Following this experience, the boy was asked to enter yet another room, where he saw a partially completed puzzle and was told this puzzle was being completed by the peer competitor. The experimenter left the boy alone with the peer's puzzle and surreptitiously videorecorded the boy's next actions.

As shown in Figure 2, two findings were clear. First, in the condition when the peer was acting with hostile intent, the boy's response was more retaliatory and aggressive than when the peer had acted ambiguously or with clearly benign intent. Second, chronically aggressive and nonaggressive boys responded differently. When the peer's intention was clearly hostile, the aggressive and nonaggressive groups of boys responded similarly with a high rate of retaliatory aggression (47% and 40%, respectively), and when the peer's intention was clearly benign, both groups responded similarly with restraint (0% retaliatory aggression for each group). But when the peer's intention was ambiguous, the chronically aggressive boys responded *as if* the peer had acted with hostile intent (20% retaliation), whereas the nonaggressive boys responded *as if* the peer had acted with benign intent (7% retaliation).

A second way to identify causality is to follow children across time. In 1987, Bates, Pettit, and I began a long-term prospective study (the Child Development

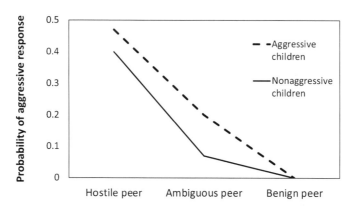

Figure 2 The relation between a peer's intention and children's retaliatory aggression: The difference between aggressive and nonaggressive children under conditions of ambiguity (adapted from Dodge, 1980).

Project, CDP) in which we identified a community sample of 585 boys and girls from three different communities (Nashville, Tennessee; Knoxville, Tennessee; and Bloomington, Indiana) in the summer before they entered kindergarten and followed them over a long period of time. Every summer, they were interviewed in their homes about their defensive mindset using the now-familiar hypothetical vignette stories of provocation, and during every school year they were observed with classmates and their parents, teachers, and peers were interviewed to identify their level of aggressive behavior. The project began when children were five years old and continues today as they reach their 40s and have children of their own. The findings provide robust support for the hypothesis that defensive mindset predicts dire outcomes.

Dodge et al. (1990) and Weiss et al. (1992) found that those children who had a defensive mindset in the summer before they entered kindergarten were more likely than other children to behave aggressively toward new peers in the kindergarten classroom. In subsequent years, Dodge et al. (1995) found that some children habitually displayed a defensive mindset every year they were interviewed across childhood. The average of their defensive mindset scores collected after preschool, kindergarten, grade 1, and grade 2 (ages 4, 5, 6, and 7, respectively) predicted their level of externalizing psychopathology during grades 3 and 4 (ages 8 and 9, respectively), even after a host of third variables that might account for this relation were controlled statistically, including children's difficult temperament in preschool, gender, and family background. These findings support the hypothesis that children with a defensive mindset escalate their future aggressive behavior problems, just as Axelrod had predicted. This pattern may seem ironic to aggressive children, who believe peers are threatening and may be trying to stop peer assaults by defending themselves, only to encounter ever increasing threats over time that require ever increasing aggressive responses. Their attributions of hostile intent become a self-fulfilling prophecy.

Causality is never proven by correlational studies, even longitudinal ones. Perhaps the most impressive empirical support for the essential hypothesis comes from the PAC cross-cultural study described earlier, because in that study, Dodge et al. (2015) controlled for children's prior level of aggressive behavior problems and tested the hypothesis in each of 12 cultures. The study was what economists call a "dif-in-dif" analysis because the early-later difference in aggressive behavior for children with high defensive mindedness was compared to the early-later difference for children with low defensive mindedness. Even after "differencing out" age-9 aggressive behavior levels, hostile attributional biases at age 10 predicted growth in children's aggressive behavior between ages 9 and 11.

2.3 How Specific Is the Relation between Hostile Attributional Bias and Problem Outcomes?

Do adverse consequences of hostile attributional bias spread to other forms of problem behavior? What about proactive bullying? What about depression? These questions have practical impact on interventions and refine our understanding of how mental processes lead to behavioral responses.

2.3.1 Hostile Attributional Bias and Reactive versus Proactive Aggressive Behavior

The first test was whether hostile attributional bias predicts both reactive aggression and instrumental (proactive) aggression. Berkowitz (1962) and Bandura (1973) argued for 60 years about whether aggressive behavior is an emotional reaction to frustration (Berkowitz) or an instrumental behavior in response to modeling and in pursuit of rewards (Bandura). The debate has been largely resolved through recognition that both scholars are correct but in different contexts: Aggression takes multiple forms, functions, etiologies, and consequences. Berkowitz studied reactive aggression, also known as impulsive aggression, intermittent explosive disorder, and retaliatory aggression. Bandura's form of aggression is less emotional and more directed at pursuit of rewards, known as instrumental aggression or proactive aggression. Hostile attributional bias should lead to reactive but not instrumental aggression.

Dodge and Coie (1987) tested this hypothesis by developing a reliable and valid teacher-rating measurement tool to assess these two forms of aggressive behavior. Although the scores for reactive and proactive aggression were positively correlated, they were able to identify five groups of boys: (1) highly reactive and highly proactive; (2) highly reactive but not proactive; (3) highly proactive but not reactive; (4) nonaggressive but still socially rejected; and (5) nonaggressive and well-functioning. They administered to all boys a new test of hostile attributional bias in which they presented videorecorded vignettes depicting provocations by one boy toward another. They asked each boy to imagine being the boy wearing a numbered t-shirt as that boy became the object of an ambiguous provocation by another boy. As depicted in Figure 3, the two groups of reactively aggressive boys were about twice as likely as the other groups to attribute hostile intent to the ambiguous provocation (left side of figure) and to react aggressively to the ambiguous provocation (right side of figure). The proactively aggressive boys did not show these patterns.

But how did these boys behave in real interactions with other boys? We created play groups in which we asked these boys to play with each other for 45 minutes on each of five consecutive days and videorecorded 551 instances

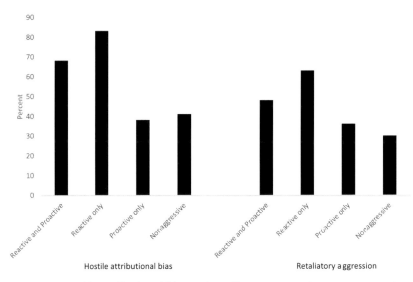

Figure 3 Hostile attributional bias and retaliatory aggression among reactive aggressive, proactive aggressive, combined aggressive, and nonaggressive children: Reactive aggressive children display hostile attributional bias (adapted from Dodge & Coie, 1987).

of overreactive aggression and 1,866 instances of proactive aggression. In between sessions, boys were interviewed to assess hostile attributional biases. True to hypotheses, a boy's hostile attributional bias tendency predicted the rate at which he displayed reactive aggressive behavior ($r = .20$, $p < .05$) but not the rate at which he displayed proactive aggression ($r = .05$, n.s.; Dodge & Coie, 1987).

By now, dozens of studies have confirmed the significant relation between hostile attributional bias and reactive, but not proactive, aggressive behavior, some by our own group (e.g., Crick & Dodge, 1996; Dodge et al., 1997; Schwartz et al., 1999) and others by independent scholars (e.g., Smithmyer et al., 2000; Walters, 2007). These studies have also shown that *other* social information processing patterns (e.g., the decision-making judgment that aggression will lead to desired outcomes) predict proactive aggressive behavior.

2.3.2 Hostile Attributional Bias and Depression

Making a hostile attribution does not inevitably lead children to react aggressively. Another mental process must follow; that is, children must also judge that reacting aggressively will lead to a positive outcome such as reducing negative internal emotion or stopping the peer from provoking again. What if children attribute hostile intent to a peer but judge that reacting aggressively would only lead to more problems?

Garber and Dodge (Garber et al., 1991; Quiggle et al., 1992) hypothesized that depressed children make hostile attributions like aggressive children do but also judge that retaliating aggressively would be foolish, and so they respond in an internalizing rather than externalizing way. This team identified four groups of children (aggressive, depressed, comorbid aggressive-and-depressed, and non-disordered) and assessed their hostile attributional biases, emotional reactions, and behavioral judgments in response to hypothetical provocations. Unique profiles of processing patterns emerged for each group. The aggressive group showed a pattern of hostile attributional bias coupled with evaluations that retaliatory aggression would be a "good" way to respond and that they could engage in aggressive retaliation rather easily (these individual social information processing patterns coalesce into an overall defensive mindset). The depressed group also showed a high level of hostile attributional bias, but they evaluated aggressive responses as a "bad" way to respond that they could not implement easily. Furthermore, they reported feeling sad when the provocation occurred and attributed the provocation to global, stable, and internal causes (that is, they infer the peer had hostile intent, but the child must have done something to cause the peer to provoke them), and they evaluated behavioral withdrawal (e.g., hiding, crying) as the best and easiest way to respond. This pattern might be called a depressive mindset. The comorbid group responded with a pattern that combined responses of the aggressive and depressed groups.

3 A General Model of Social Information Processing

Findings like those reported above indicate the relation between hostile attributions and problem behavior is rule-governed with many contingencies. Although hostile attributional bias is a fundamental (almost necessary) process in reactive aggressive behavior, it does not explain proactive aggressive behavior such as bullying and armed robbery. Also, a hostile attributional bias does not inevitably lead to reactive aggression; it might instead lead to depressive withdrawal. How can we predict the way children will behave when they make a hostile attribution? It became clear we need a more comprehensive model of all the mental processes invoked in real time during social interactions. The following section presents a general model of social information processing.

The most general model of how humans solve problems was developed by Simon (1967). His work addressed the decisions made by corporate administrators, but he also considered other social and non-social situations, including chess-playing. The essence of Simon's contribution to economics was to assert that humans solve problems in real time through a sequence of mental actions in which the person is presented a given problem and a goal, considers one or more possible decisions and the likely consequences or goodness-of-fit of each possible decision, and then selects the decision that has the highest probability of a desired outcome. His model improved upon economic models of the day by incorporating both rational and irrational factors and has been cited as the basis for artificial intelligence (Donovan, 2023).

Simon's model addresses a fundamental human system, similar to the respiratory system and the digestive system. These systems have in common several features. They serve an essential function in keeping humans alive and in growing the person over time and across development. They are dynamically interactive with the environment. They act in real time to receive input (such as air or food), process that input to extract essential human resources (such as oxygen or nutrients), and respond with exertion of energy. So, too, there must be a "social information processing" system that functions to keep the human alive and to grow emotionally. That system receives social input, processes it to extract meaning, and responds with exertion of social energy. Most of the time, these systems function smoothly, and humans breathe freely, grow physically, and interact in fulfilling social relationships. But some of the time in every person, or a lot of the time in some persons, the system fails, and the person cannot breathe, chokes on food, or becomes lost emotionally.

> *"The central nervous system is a serial information processor that must serve an organism endowed with multiple needs, and living in an environment that presents unpredictable threats and opportunities. (Simon, 1967, p. 29)."*

Simon's statement addresses several essential components of a full social information processing system. "Central nervous system" means the system is brain driven (i.e., mental) but reaches through the whole body. "Serial information processor" means the brain engages in a sequence of distinct mental steps in serial fashion in real time. "Multiple needs" implies an array of possible goals. "Unpredictable threats and opportunities" imply the system serves both negative and positive forces that require ongoing vigilance and suggest the emotional volatility of goals.

Over time, I articulated a general social information processing model (Dodge, 1986), deepened it with Crick (Crick & Dodge, 1994), broadened it with Pettit (Dodge & Pettit, 2003), and evolved it following empirical inquiry (Dodge, 2006). It is depicted in Figure 4, which shows that children come to a social situation with biological capabilities and a history of experiences that

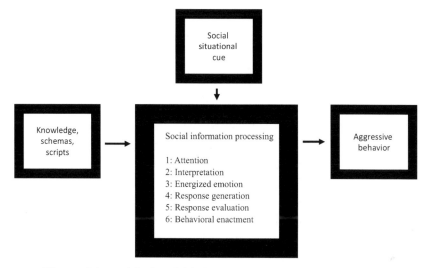

Figure 4 A model of social information processing (adapted from Dodge, 2006).

guides their progression through social information processing steps to lead to a behavioral response. Although actual responding occurs in discrete steps in real time, a child's overall pattern of responding across all components of social information processing can be characterized as a mindset. This Element is about the defensive mindset, but other patterns can be identified such as the helpless (depressive) mindset, the learning (versus performance) mindset, the altruistic mindset, and the competitive mindset.

3.1 Social Knowledge

Before children respond in real time during social interactions, they come to a social encounter with a set of biologically endowed capabilities and a history of prior social experiences. The capabilities are sensory programs that have been honed since birth (or before), such as vision and hearing, as well as intellectual and behavioral skills. Compared with most other species, human infants are born helpless (e.g., horses are born walking). They are highly dependent upon caregivers for survival and require environmental experience to acquire behavioral skill. The utter helplessness of human infants applies less to respiration and digestion and more to emotional comfort. We are social creatures and depend on social connections to survive.

The history of experiences stored in the brain is not a veridical map of actual experiences but rather a template of interpreted experiences that Huesmann (1988) has called schemas of social concepts, scripts of how behavior is played out, and knowledge about social encounters. This social knowledge guides children's processing of information in future encounters, and the outcomes of those encounters are then iteratively integrated into memory to update social knowledge. People do not store in memory a literal "photo" or "film" of their encounters with others. Such memory films would rapidly run into millions of disorganized files that could not be called on easily in future interactions. So people develop heuristic "short cut" narratives that get stored in memory. Schemas and scripts mapped in memory are unique to each person and are constantly growing and evolving with every new encounter. Beginning at birth, millions of neural synapses are associations laid down every second following each social experience. For example, the infant learns: "See mother, feel comfort." Or perhaps another infant learns: "See mother's boyfriend, feel fear."

Psychologists have created instruments to assess children's social knowledge, schemas, and scripts. Huesmann and Guerra (1997) have shown through a series of empirical studies that individual differences in children's normative beliefs about aggression predict aggressive behavior problems in children and adolescents. Our lab team has distinguished between beliefs legitimizing aggression (as Huesmann and Guerra would measure) and online processing actions (such as attributions) and tested the relation between social knowledge and aggressive behavior in three large, independent samples.

First, Zelli et al. (1999) presented instruments measuring beliefs about aggression and other instruments measuring social information processing patterns to children in a longitudinal panel called the Fast Track (FT) study (to be described later) and found that children's positive beliefs about aggression predict their development of aggressive behavior problems and that this relation is partially mediated by the characteristic ways children process social cues. That is, children who hold favorable beliefs and have refined knowledge about aggression are likely to attribute hostile intent to others and to evaluate aggressive behaviors as having positive consequences, which, in turn, predict their development of aggressive behavior.

With an independent sample of children in the Social Development Project (SDP), Burks et al. (1999a) assessed children's social knowledge by asking them to talk about peers they knew in an open-ended way. They scored the valenced content of children's stories about peers, the density of their knowledge about aggression (breadth, complexity, and fluency), and the accessibility of their aggressive constructs. All of these measures of social knowledge predicted children's level of teacher-rated aggressive behavior problems both concurrently and several years into the future.

With the children of the Child Development Project (CDP), Burks et al. (1999b) asked children to engage in a sentence completion task (e.g., "My father ... ") and coded the hostility of their mental constructs and used an assessment of schema typicality to score the hostility of their schemas. Children with more hostile schemas and higher levels of hostile mental constructs had higher levels of externalizing behavior problems as rated by teachers and mothers.

3.2 Steps of Social Information Processing

The social information processing (SIP) model in Figure 4 is a heuristic description of mental action steps that occur in real time in response to a specific social stimulus and that lead to a social behavioral response. It is a model of competent performance; that is, competent and successful responding follows these steps. Failure to engage in a particular step or incompetent responding at a step could lead to behavioral failure. The mental steps together predict the behavioral response. People engage in these mental steps during each social encounter, and across development they adopt somewhat consistent ways of responding, to the extent that stimuli are similar. These consistent responses constitute acquired individual differences in social information processing that predict individual differences in general behavioral tendencies.

3.2.1 Step 1: Attention

As a social stimulus presents itself, the child's first step of processing is to attend to the social cues. There are literally millions of cues in an environment at any moment, far too many for any person to encode. And cues change with each passing moment. Humans have evolved over millennia so that social encounters take priority and capture particular attention, from the moment of birth when an infant begins to focus on their mother and interpret her smile as comforting. As the initial process through which children encounter a social stimulus, attention influences all downstream processes. It is easy to contemplate the impact that attending to a peer's face and the peer's look of surprise (or malice) will have on the way children respond to being bumped by a peer. Both within- and between-child differences predict behavioral responding.

Because there is no such thing as an eidetic (photographic) social memory store, people have evolved to use common heuristics to code the stimulus: "Focus on the other person's face," "Attend to tone of voice as much as the words," "Create a narrative that has meaning and store in memory the narrative rather than the individual parts." One can easily imagine children's occasional missteps in which they fail to pay proper attention due to fatigue, preoccupation, or random error; and one can imagine the success that follows when children consciously bring their eyes into "focus" on a particular task.

Between-child differences are also important. People develop heuristics that are unique to their own experience: "Be wary of rapid movements." "Look for the other's weak spot." "Find the good in others." In rapid time, people encode stimuli into the brain in their unique way. Clear and obvious cues are coded similarly by most people, but, as the cue becomes more ambiguous, individual differences play an increasing role. Some differences are a function of acquired skill, and others are a function of unique experiences that bias attention. Simon (1967) showed that chess masters are expert at noticing an opponent's early attempts to set up a later attack on the king. One child might have acquired exquisite skill at detecting another's facial movements (perhaps through numerous past emotional encounters), whereas another child may be oblivious. We know these patterns as "selective attention," "biased attention," "hypervigilance," "attentiveness," and "attention deficits."

In the CDP sample, Dodge et al. (1995) scored children's open-ended responses to each of 24 provocation vignettes as indicating attention to relevant social cues (or not). As hypothesized, the sum score for lack of attention to relevant cues predicted higher teacher-rated aggression on the Child Behavior Checklist and more classroom peer nominations for being an aggressive behavior problem (Dodge et al., 1995). Dodge and Price (1994) replicated these findings with the SDP sample. Once again, children's scores for lack of attention to relevant social cues predicted both higher teacher ratings and more peer nominations. A feature of the SDP sample was the different ages of children (6, 7, or 8), enabling a demonstration that attention to relevant cues improves with each advancing year and the correlation between attention scores and children's aggressive behavior increases as children get older.

Other investigators have created different ways of measuring children's selective or biased attention (such as distraction and total attentive capacity) to social cues. Gouze (1987) asked 4- and 5-year-old boys to pay attention to a video screen that alternately displayed 12 short vignettes in which two puppets were either fighting with each other or sharing with each other, and to press a button as quickly as possible when a red light turned on in the corner of the screen. The average latency of pressing the button while the puppets were fighting, minus the average latency of responding while the puppets were sharing, was an indication of hyper-attention to aggressive stimuli. These children were then observed on the playground for at least 50 minutes each. A boy's hyper-attention-to-aggression score predicted a higher rate of physically aggressing against peers. Heightened focus on aggression and threat by others is the first processing step in the pattern of defensive mindedness.

3.2.2 Step 2: Interpretation

As cues are encoded in the brain, they get interpreted. People have evolved to interpret social cues along specific dimensions that foster survival (is the cue a threat?), security (is the cue calming?), and growth (does the cue indicate an opportunity?).

The most basic dimension of interpretation is threat versus no threat. Infants initially interpret all disruptive cues (e.g., a loud sound, sudden movement) as threat (not consciously, but instinctively) and respond with crying, a facial expression of fear, and a psychophysiological stress response. As infants grow and gain experience, they learn to distinguish actual threats from "accidents" or non-threats, typically by age three or four. A unique characteristic of humans is the ability to imagine, guess, or interpret the intentions of another person, commonly called "theory of mind." Many animals have information processing systems that include interpretation of another animal's cues as threatening or not; only humans can contemplate that the other can have intentions. We learn that not all disruptive cues are intentional threats; sometimes, the other person causes a bad outcome for us inadvertently through an accident or even for a good intention (e.g., a physician gives a painful shot to a child to provide immunization). The distinction between another's intentions and outcomes is hard for young children to realize but an important lesson to learn.

Both skills and biases differentiate across children. Not all children learn the skill of accurate interpretation at the same pace. Particularly important are skills of recognizing different emotions, both in other people and in the self. Five-year-old children readily recognize when another person is displaying a positive emotion ("good") versus a negative emotion ("bad"), but they have only a rudimentary ability to recognize the differences among negative emotions (e.g., "sad" versus "mad"). Their interpretation of their own internal cues (such as the meaning of an accelerating heart rate) is also developing during early childhood.

Innate tendencies and specific socializing experiences lead children to acquire unique heuristic biases in interpretation. Poor Charlie Brown always interpreted Lucy's words as indicating she would benignly hold the football in place while he tried to kick it; he was always surprised when she picked up the ball as his toe came close to touching it. At the other extreme, early adverse experiences lead some children to become biased toward interpreting others' intentions as hostile.

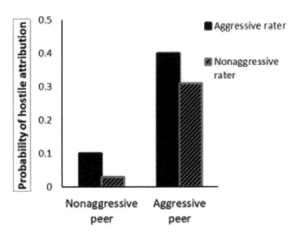

Figure 5 Hostile attributional biases by and toward aggressive children
(adapted from Dodge, 1980).

As with attention, numerous constructs are captured by this processing step, depending on the stimulus, including attribution of another's intention under conditions of ambiguity, skill of interpreting another's intention accurately under conditions of clarity, and skill at recognizing another's emotional state. All three constructs have been associated with children's aggressive behavioral problems.

The most replicated finding is the association between a bias to make an attribution of hostile intent and aggressive behavior problems. As I described in my dissertation study (Dodge, 1980), I presented hypothetical cartoon stories to aggressive and nonaggressive boys in which they imagined being the object of an ambiguous provocation by a named classroom peer, who was known to be aggressive or nonaggressive. As Figure 5 depicts, the aggressive group had a .25 probability of attributing hostile intent to the peer, in contrast with a significantly lower probability of .17 for the nonaggressive group. The bias held both when the peer was a known aggressive boy and when the peer was a known nonaggressive boy, it held across all ages studied (7, 9, and 11), and the magnitude of effect increased as boys got older.

One hypothesis was not supported: I speculated that if aggressive boys are simply disorganized, the magnitude of the association between their attribution of intent and their behavioral response would be smaller than that for nonaggressive boys. No evidence emerged to support this hypothesis, indicating that the processing pattern displayed by aggressive boys is rule-governed and biased rather than arbitrary and disorganized.

To enhance the realism of the stimuli, Dodge et al. (1986) videorecorded six vignettes with child actors in which one child actor ambiguously provoked another child (e.g., knocked his puzzle over). Child research participants watched the vignettes and made interpretations about the provocateur's intentions. Later, the same children were asked to play with unacquainted peers (who were in fact child actors), in which one peer ambiguously knocked over the child's puzzle. The rate at which a child attributed hostile intent to the video stimuli predicted the likelihood that the child would react to an actual provocation with retaliatory aggression. Since those first studies, over 400 published reports have replicated the basic finding. At least three meta-analyses (Orbio de Castro et al., 2002; Tuente et al., 2019; Verhoef et al., 2019) concluded the finding is robust, not accountable by any third variable, and shows a pattern of hostile attributions driving reactive aggressive behavior.

Are aggressive children less accurate than others at identifying others intentions? The second interpretation construct is accuracy at detecting others' intentions. Dodge et al. (1984) created 300 videorecorded vignettes, each depicting a provocation in which the peer actor's intent varied as: (1) hostile; (2) prosocial; (3) accidental or benign; (4) ambiguous; or (5) merely present, that is not involved at all in the provocation. Socially rejected, aggressive behavior-problem children were less accurate than average and popular non-aggressive children overall. To replicate the findings, Dodge et al. (1986) presented six of the vignettes (two prosocial intent, two hostile intent, and two accidental) to aggressive children and matched nonaggressive children and found the nonaggressive children were more accurate than aggressive children at identifying prosocial intent, whereas the aggressive children were more accurate than the nonaggressive children at detecting truly hostile intent.

The third construct in this processing step is emotion recognition. It is so important to learn to recognize emotions in others to get along with them and in recognizing one's own emotions to regulate them. Many young children can tell whether they are feeling "good" versus "bad" but are not able to tell whether their bad feeling is "sad" or "mad." Numerous investigators have created instruments to assess emotion recognition. One of the most-used instruments is a set of photographs developed by Tottenham depicting facial expressions of different emotions (Tottenham et al., 2009). Acland et al. (2023) presented photographs depicting happiness, sadness, anger, and fear to assess children's skills at accurately recognizing emotions. The findings are clear: aggressive children are less accurate than other children at recognizing fear and sadness in others' faces. Schwenck and colleagues (2014) created a morphing task in which clinically diagnosed conduct-disordered girls (without callous-unemotional traits, meaning they were likely reactively aggressive rather than cold bullies) and matched controls were presented 60 film clips, each 9 seconds long, in which a neutral face gradually morphed into a face expressing a particular emotion. Girls were asked to press a key as soon as they recognized the emotion and to label it. The conduct-disordered girls were slower than the controls to recognize happy, sad, and fearful faces, but not slower to recognize anger. They were also less accurate than the controls at recognizing sadness and fear but not anger.

Dodge et al. (2002) administered Ribordy et al.'s (1988) Emotion Recognition Questionnaire instrument, in which the interviewer presented each of 16 situational vignettes about an episode that happened to another child (four each depicting each of fear, sadness, anger, and happiness) and asked children to identify the emotion the peer was experiencing. Poorer accuracy in identifying fear and sadness predicted children's aggressive behavior problems as rated by both parents and classroom teachers.

It is important not only to recognize emotions in others but also to recognize emotions in oneself. Greenberg and Kusche (1993) developed the Interview of Emotional Experience to ascertain the emotions children report they would experience in response to situations that normally elicit different emotions of fear, sadness, anger, and happiness. With the Fast Track sample, Dodge et al. (2002) found that problems in recognizing sadness and fear in oneself predicted children's aggressive behavior problems.

3.2.3 Step 3: Energized Emotional Experience

Through neural associations potentiated across generations and laid down through acquired experiences, interpretation of social cues ignites emotional reactions. Phenomenologically, when we interpret a social cue, we construct an emotional response, perhaps fear, joy, anxiety, or anger. There is considerable debate in the science of emotion about whether emotions are prewired responses to specific cues or are dynamically constructed during social interaction (Rosen & Levenson, 2009). Either way, an emotion is not merely a passive and epiphenomenal event: It is accompanied by whole bodily reactions. Emotions are neural calls to action. Upon interpreting a social cue, the prefrontal cortex signals other regions of the brain (through neural synapses) and the peripheral nervous system to secrete testosterone, release cortisol into the bloodstream, change the heart's rate of beating, and alter breathing, depending on the interpretation.

Those neural pathways follow general human maps but also form large individual differences. The same interpretation of a cue (perhaps as a threat) could trigger anger in one child and paralyzing hopeless fear in another child. Emotions motivate behavior; without emotion, we wither. The function of an emotion is to set an energized direction for a behavioral response, which we call

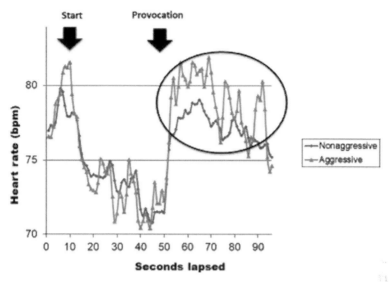

Figure 6 Mean second-by-second heart rate reactivity in response to provocation for aggressive and nonaggressive boys (adapted from Crozier et al., 2008).

a goal. Goals and goal-setting (even unconsciously) are thus essential parts of this step of processing.

Rose and Asher (1999) presented hypothetical social conflict situations to children and asked them what their goal would be if the conflict happened to them. Children who consistently generated a goal of "revenge" toward others, even toward their own friends, had the most problems in relating to peers, including aggression.

In our lab, Crozier and colleagues (2008) led a study of the effect of experienced provocation on the sympathetic nervous system. We brought CDP participants into the laboratory and tracked children's heart rate while the children watched videorecorded vignettes and answered questions. The average profile of heart rate changed while children watched the vignettes, as shown in Figure 6. As the interviewer told the children to anticipate the beginning of a video, their average heart rate increased, but when the video began, their heart rate declined as they attended to the story. This decline in heart rate as children focus attention is a well-documented response pattern. At the moment the video depicted a provocation (such as the focal child being bumped in the back), children's heart rates soared. Over time, heart rates returned to baseline. This pattern of cardiac response to provocation (sharp increase followed by gradual return to baseline) held for both aggressive and nonaggressive children, but two differences were apparent, particularly among boys. First, aggressive children, relative to nonaggressive children, responded with greater psychophysiological reactivity (higher spikes in heart rate) immediately following the presentation of the provocation. Second, their return to heart rate baseline took longer. Further analyses indicated that children who responded with these two patterns of heart rate reactivity (high spike following provocation and long lag until return to baseline) also displayed biased social information processing responses. The combined psychophysiological and mental responses indicate a defensive mindset.

Also in our lab, Carré et al. (2014) studied the effect of experienced provocation on the endocrine system. The hypothalamic–pituitary–gonadal (HPG) axis, and its hormonal end product testosterone, is associated with aggressive behavior. In particular, acute fluctuations in the release of testosterone during social interactions predict aggressive responding. We hypothesized that rapid testosterone release (measured from saliva samples) would be part of the whole-body defensive mindset response pattern. Carré et al. brought into the laboratory the Durham participants in the Fast Track study and asked participants to play a computer game with a peer who was in another room. There was no actual peer; rather, Carré et al. simulated the peer's responses. The goal of the game was to earn points by pressing a button as rapidly as possible or by "stealing" points from the peer by pressing a different button. Throughout the game, points were "stolen" from the participant by the peer at random intervals. Carré et al. collected saliva samples from the participants before they began the game and after each of three 10-minute intervals. As expected, following the initial provocation by the fictitious peer, testosterone levels increased by 7% (among participants who had not experienced clinical intervention). Second, a higher magnitude of testosterone increase predicted the participants' higher rate of reactive aggressive behavior (stealing points) toward the peer. Third, the group of participants who had been randomly assigned to receive the Fast Track intervention showed a pattern of less release of testosterone in response to provocation and less reactive aggressive behavior toward the peer (see Section 6 on intervention).

3.2.4 Step 4: Response Generation

Once children interpret social cues and experience emotions and goals, one or more possible behavioral responses is called to mind from a memory bin of behaviors. Investigators have called this process "response generation" when it occurs outside of consciousness and "social problem solving" when it is a conscious act, and they have measured both the number of responses children generate and the quality of those responses. Hundreds of studies have shown that children who generate fewer assertive and more aggressive solutions than do average peers are relatively likely to develop aggressive behavior problems.

Dodge et al. (1986) assessed children's response generation patterns in several kinds of situations. They began with a non-conflict situational task, trying to initiate entry into a group of peers already at play, by creating video vignettes of unacquainted peers at play and asking each child, "Tell me all the ways you could get other kids to let you join their group." Later, they brought each child to a different room where two strange peers were already at play on a puzzle and asked the child to try to join the group, and they coded children's peer group entry strategy behaviors. Dodge et al. were able to predict children's actual likelihood of behavioral success in joining the peer group based on the proportion of responses to the problem-solving task that were aggressive and scored as incompetent, as well as the total number of solutions they generated. Next, Dodge et al. presented hypothetical provocations to children and asked them to generate possible responses to being provoked. In a separate session, they brought the same children into the laboratory to play with an unacquainted peer (actually, a child actor) who provoked them, and they observed children's actual behavioral response. They found that the more reactive aggressive behavior responses children generated in the problem-solving task, the greater the likelihood that children reacted aggressively when actually provoked.

Bookhout et al. (2021) expanded on these assessments with novel stimuli and research methods. They asked children to imagine being provoked by a peer and to generate possible responses. They found a positive correlation between the number of aggressive responses a child generated and directly observed rates of aggressive rule-breaking behavior on the playground.

3.2.5 *Step 5: Response Evaluation and Decision Making*

Not every behavioral response that is called up from memory gets enacted. Thankfully, children learn the ability to withhold an impulse. Children might feel anger and have an impulse to hit back (or grab a candy bar off the shelf of a store or spit on a baby brother), but people develop the capability to hold in mind a possible response and evaluate it before making a decision to act upon it. We learn impulse control. People also develop the ability to observe themselves before responding, called "executive function." This step of processing is a major component of emotion regulation.

Fontaine and Dodge (2006) articulated a formal model of response evaluation and decision making (RED) in real time. The model proposes the idea of minimal acceptability threshold; that is, a possible behavior that is called to mind (such as hitting a peer in the head) is quickly evaluated by the brain for acceptability; if the response is above a minimum threshold, it is selected for enactment. If it is below threshold, the person seeks an alternative response. Numerous factors may push this threshold downward, such as high blood alcohol level, fatigue, angry mood, or a general dispositional propensity to act quickly. Other factors may push the threshold upward, such as authority figures who are ready to pounce on one's mistake. Fontaine and Dodge also asserted that the threshold is higher at the beginning of a social interchange, and if no generated response reaches the minimally acceptable threshold, a child might "lower the standard" and resort to a response that had previously been evaluated as unacceptable.

How does a child decide whether a response is above threshold of acceptability in expected outcome? It is a risk-reward calculation. Fontaine identifies many domains of outcomes that children could consider in making a decision, including instrumental consequences ("Will I get my ball back?"), social consequences ("Will they like me?"), intrapersonal consequences ("Will I feel good inside myself?"), and moral consequences ("Is this what I believe is right?"). Not only are the expected consequences evaluated, but each consequence is given a valuation. Children might consider that a behavior will cause others to dislike them but might not care much about that consequence.

In real time, children consider the likely evaluated and valuated consequences of each generated possible response in each of multiple relevant domains, do some mental calculus, and select the best response for implementation. If no response exceeds a minimal threshold of acceptability, children might go back to the memory bin for more possible solutions, experienced as "thinking" and problem solving. Fontaine hypothesized a mathematical formula to guide decision making, in which children (not consciously, maybe not even in reality but heuristically) compute an acceptability score for a possible behavioral response that is the sum of the various evaluated consequences, weighted by the value given to each consequence.

Fontaine and Dodge represented the evaluation process as:

$$OS_i = Oe_i * Ov_i,$$

where OS_i is the overall acceptability score for outcome i, and is a function of Oe_i which is the expectancy score for outcome i multiplied by Ov_i which is the valuation score for outcome i.

In a study of 259 adolescents, Fontaine et al. (2002) found that children's positive evaluations of aggressive responses, negative evaluations of nonaggressive responses, and high valuations of self-serving consequences predicted heightened levels of aggressive behavior problems. In a replication with the CDP sample, Fontaine et al. (2008) found that these aggressogenic RED processes predict the growth of aggressive behavior across adolescence.

One general decision-making heuristic that has been hypothesized to characterize aggressive children is the overvaluation of immediate outcomes to the neglect of long-term outcomes. One may be familiar with Mischel's "marshmallow test" in which young children are presented with a choice to grab one marshmallow immediately or multiple marshmallows later if they can wait a short period of time. So, too, during certain social encounters, some children inordinately value immediate consequences (e.g., hitting a peer who is playing with a child's toy) over longer-term consequences (e.g., staying out of trouble with the teacher). Economists call the tendency to prioritize immediate consequences "delay discounting."

Delay discounting is not always a conscious, reasoned decision by a rational child. Perhaps we all can gain some degree of empathy or at least insight if we see a similarity between children's impulsive hitting and adults' problems with impulse control in certain situations. Even the best of us sometimes caves into the temptation of a piece of chocolate cake. We know we should not take that bite, but in one fleeting moment the allure of the taste is so powerful we ignore consideration of later costs. Alcoholics face this problem each time they see a drink. Cigarette smokers know they should quit, but when they smell smoke or are stressed, they tell lies to themselves that one more cigarette will not kill them. These are otherwise responsible adults who fall down in certain situations. Why should aggressive children be any different?

Economists may have labeled the phenomenon of delay discounting, but psychologists have identified life experiences and eras that control it. Belsky (2014) hypothesized that early life experiences of severe and constant threat predispose children to accelerate pubertal timing and to discount long-term consequences, partly because their "long-term" may never come to pass if they die before growing up. Kotlowitz (1991) recounted an interview with children on the south side of Chicago who told him, "If I grow up, I'd like to be a bus driver." Kotlowitz recounted the narrative as: "*If*, not *when*." No doubt this schema about life influences the child's mental calculus about whether to invest in homework or after-school play. In a study of many cultures around the world, Steinberg et al. (2018) identified an era during biological adolescence when teenagers' immediate reward calculations go berserk: "I want, I want, I want."

Impulsive responding without considering consequences at all and over-consideration of rewards (and the complementary neglect of consideration of punishment) are two additional components of decision making that predict children's aggressive behavior problems. In our lab, Yechiam et al. (2006)

proposed and tested a formal model of responding to laboratory gambling tasks (known as "go no-go" or passive avoidance tasks). In one task, the child is presented a series of numbers on a screen and is asked each time to press a button if the number is "good." If correct, the child receives 25 cents. If the child presses a button for a "bad" number, the child loses 25 cents. The child receives neither punishment nor reward for not pressing a button. Across 90 trials, Yechiam et al. (2006) scored the child's responsiveness to rewards (button pressing for good numbers to receive 25 cents) and impulsivity (errors of commission when the child should have withheld button-pressing in response to bad numbers) and found that each factor predicted both teacher- and self-reports of externalizing behavior problems, even controlling for intelligence and family income.

3.2.6 Step 6: Behavioral Enactment

Ultimately, a child selects a behavioral response. The final step in processing is to transform a selected behavioral response into behavioral actions. This step might seem trivial, but important motor and verbal skills are involved and factors such as anxiety can impair performance. Children might decide on an assertive behavioral response (e.g., in response to a bullying peer who took the child's bicycle for a ride, the child might decide to ask for the bike back), but meek performance could reduce the likelihood the behavior reaches its goal. Modeling of behavior, rehearsal, and practice can improve the ease of behavioral enactment and lead to more rapid and relaxed performance. Individual differences in enactment skill may be large and could determine success.

Relatively few studies have examined this step. Dodge et al. (1986) brought aggressive and nonaggressive children into the laboratory for interviews, during which the interviewer asked children to act out different ways of responding. For example, for each of four hypothetical peer group entry situations, the interviewer said,

> "*One way you could get others to play with you is to ask them. Let's pretend that I am seated at the table and you would like to play with me. Show me how you would ask me if you could play with me.*"

For each of four provocation situations, children were asked to enact a competent-assertive response to being provoked, such as asking a peer to return a toy they had taken from the child. The idea was to control all decisions about what behavior to enact and to focus solely on behavioral and verbal skills. Children's competence in enacting each response was scored by the interviewer on a 5-point scale. The aggressive group was rated as less competent at enacting competent-assertive responses than the nonaggressive group.

3.3 Cumulative Prediction from All Steps

The SIP model asserts that, although children's processing responses across different measures at different steps of processing may be correlated with each other (e.g., hypervigilant responses may be positively correlated with hostile attributional biases), responses at each step provide unique information about the child's mental processes and incremental prediction of that child's behavior. That is, the strength of the prediction of aggressive behavior will be greater from the combined profile of all processing measures than from any single measure. One can test this hypothesis by assessing all steps of processing within a child and then applying stepwise regression models to evaluate whether processing responses across steps are redundant or unique-and-incremental in predicting aggressive behavior problems.

In numerous independent studies, the unique-and-incremental hypothesis has won out. Dodge et al. (1986) found that responses at each of four different steps of processing about provocations increased the prediction accuracy of children's aggressive behavior in response to provocations as directly observed and as rated by teachers. With a separate sample of children, Dodge et al. (1986) found similarly that each of four processing patterns about peer group entry increased the prediction accuracy of children's actual peer group entry competence.

Dodge and Price (1994) replicated these findings with the SDP sample in both provocation and peer entry situations and extended them to a third kind of situation, responding to ambiguous demands by authority figures (e.g., a teacher says, "Come to my desk, immediately.") For each of the three kinds of situations, processing patterns at each step of processing provided unique increments in predicting aggressive behavior and behavioral competence in that kind of situation. Yet other replications came from studies with the Fast Track sample and the CDP sample (Dodge et al., 2002).

3.4 Integration of Social Information Processing Steps into a Primal Concept of Defensive Mindset

The findings that aggressive children display many divergent social information processing deficits imply that to understand fully the development of aggressive behavior problems, we might need dozens of disparate mental constructs and measures of processing patterns about many different types of situations and with many different peer relationships. Indeed, regression analyses suggest that each processing step in each situation adds unique information to understanding children's aggressive behavior problems. The implications from this work for intervention with aggressive children could be even more daunting: If intervention to reduce children's aggressive behavior must address each processing construct in each type of situation separately, it would take an awfully long time to penetrate children's psyche. My experience in intervention with chronically aggressive school children, however, suggested positive spillovers during intervention. For example, successfully showing a child that a benign attribution of intent is just as plausible as a hostile attribution (at Step 2 of processing) could lead that child to become more attentive to benign cues in future interactions (at Step 1). Also, helping a child realize the negative long-term consequences of retaliating aggressively are not worth any short-term reward (at Step 5 of processing) could lead that child to generate alternatives to retaliation (at Step 4).

To buttress the case based on empirical studies, the findings reviewed in Section 3.3 show measures of defensive processing are significantly correlated with each other, such that they might be aggregated into a single coherent measure of a defensive mindset construct. Using the Fast Track participants in early elementary school, Dodge et al. (2002) showed the psychometric soundness of aggregating the disparate processing scores into a single latent construct. These analyses provided support for the unique-and-incremental hypothesis, but they also provide support for multidimensional latent constructs of defensive mindset in each situation that predict aggressive behavior problems within that type of situation. The findings proved robust but nuanced, supporting the paradox of two general hypotheses:

1) Measures of different steps of processing uniquely increment to predict behavior in a situation such that the aggregated profile provides the strongest prediction;

and

2) Measures of different steps of processing in a situation are correlated with each other to form a reliable latent construct of defensive mindset.

Taken together, these hypotheses suggest a nested model in which responses within a step of processing are highly intercorrelated and are empirically distinguished from responses at other steps (supporting the construct validity of each processing step), but latent constructs at each step are intercorrelated as well (supporting the construct validity of an overall defensive mindset). Dodge et al. (2022) tested empirical fit to a hypothesized model of social information processing steps nested within a broader defensive mindset using data from the Fast Track study that had been collected across ages 5 to 16. The data fit each of four independent social information processing latent constructs, and these four processing patterns fit a fifth, higher-order latent construct of a defensive mindset. The first latent variable was indicated by three variables measuring hypervigilant selective attention. The second latent variable was indicated by seven variables measuring hostile attributional bias. The third latent variable was indicated by seven variables measuring aggressive response generation. The fourth latent variable was indicated by four variables measuring positive aggressive response evaluation. The fifth latent variable, overall defensive mindset, was indicated by the four latent variables. A latent variable for emotional response was not tested because of insufficient data. Model fit statistics supported the hypothesized nested model. To be sure the findings had not inadvertently capitalized on chance, Dodge et al. (2022) replicated the same analyses with the children of the CDP and found similar results.

This work represents a dramatic transformation in how I conceptualize social information processing. At first, each processing measure was thought of as uniquely and independently formed from a history of different specific experiences that were unrelated to each other. They could be summed into an index, but the index did not presume that the mental processes originated from the same past experience or source. This conceptualization implies a number of independent measurements that could sum to a total score with arrows of "cause" going from each measurement to the summed score, as in the top half of Figure 7.

The transformation is to reverse the direction of the arrows. An underlying mental construct, call it a "primal construct," is accumulated from a life history of experiences that are stored in memory and "cause" children's social knowledge structures, which, in turn, guide how children process social information at each step of a social interaction. A single latent construct is not sufficient; however, children also learn from situation-specific histories as well as histories at each processing step, in a nested model. The revised model is depicted in the bottom half of Figure 7.

Figure 8 summarizes major factors that reflect defensive mindset from the many studies reviewed here.

4 Life Course Outcomes of Defensive Mindset

One of the most vexing characteristics of a defensive mindset is that it does not typically go away on its own. Many other "problems" in childhood spontaneously remit as biological maturation takes over, self-correction brings children back on course, or children's caregivers provide positive and remedial experiences to support them. If you are a parent, think about your different children

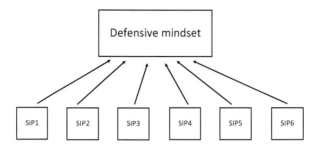

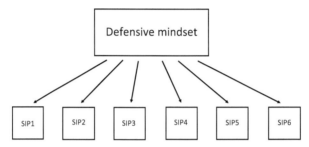

Figure 7 Defensive mindset as a manifest sum of independent processing actions versus a primal latent construct (adapted from Dodge et al., 2022).

and their experiences at different ages. When one child developed a problem, such as a decline in grades at school, you probably jumped into action to address the problem through extra homework or tutoring until the problem abated. Your efforts in response to a problem relieved the problem rather than exacerbating it.

Not so with a defensive mindset. The story is more one of self-fulfilling prophecy. Defensively minded children expect others to threaten them, harm them, and exclude them, and so they preemptively act as if those responses from others are already happening. Defensively minded children enter the room with their fists already clenched, so to speak, and walk around with a scowl, looking for a conflict. So what happens? Conflicts ensue. Peers act aggressively toward them. Teachers scowl back. The situation is tragic. These children misinterpret innocent peer intentions and respond with aggressive behaviors that they believe are justified and retaliatory-in-kind rather than instigative. Peers don't see the situation in the same way, however. They see these children's aggressive behavior as unwarranted and respond with justified retaliation of their own. Defensively minded children observe peers' reactions and think to themselves,

"See, I was right. They are mean to me." These children's initial expectations that others will be hostile have been positively reinforced, and the neural pathway in the brain between a peer provocation stimulus and a hostile attribution has been strengthened.

Patterson (1976) called this pattern a "coercive cycle" that reminded him of a vortex, or whirlpool, which captures the child and everyone in shouting distance. Once the vortex starts swirling, talking and persuasion do little to calm the waters. Patterson applied the vortex to parent–child interactions, but it applies equally well to child–peer interactions. These children's own experiences convince them that they are right and they need to be vigilant, and so defensive mindedness becomes their identity. Others around them observe these children and are convinced their stereotype is right, and so they exclude and rebuff them. The vortex grows.

Our longitudinal studies suggest three stages of escalation across the life course that characterize defensively minded children's problems, starting with how these problems *cascade* as parents, teachers, and peers give up on the defensive child. In young adulthood, the defensive-minded individual sadly *fails in life tasks*, as the risks of loneliness, unemployment, psychopathology, and violent crime are high. Finally, in later life, the defensive person is at risk of *premature death*. The defensive-minded youngster is four times more likely than other persons to die before reaching age 50.

4.1 Defensive Mindset Cascades into "Giving Up" in Adolescence

As defensive-minded children become adolescents, their problems often cascade into deeper aggressive behavior and a wider array of problems that could include greater parent–child conflict, substance abuse, school failure, violent behavior in romantic relationships, and involvement in the criminal justice system. These predictions are probabilistic, and the reader should not infer determinism because intervening life events might deflect a child's trajectory; indeed, the hope of intervention is precisely to deflect children from a vector of tragedy.

With the CDP sample, Lansford et al. (2006) assessed defensive mindset as early as the summer prior to kindergarten at age 4, followed children for 12 years, and found early defensive mindset scores predicted heightened mother-reported externalizing psychopathology (a broad psychiatric disorder that encompasses antisocial behavior, substance use, aggression, and interpersonally aversive and challenging personality disorders such as psychopathy and narcissism) at age 17. How does this cascade happen, and why is there a turn for the worse in adolescence?

Social knowledge and preoccupation with aggression and threat

Memories of past events characterized by threat

Schematic organization of memories by the construct of threat

Mental scripts for social interaction characterized by threat and retaliation

Dense knowledge of aggressive behavior

Social information processing steps

1. ***Hypervigilance to threat***

    Selective attention to threat cues in the environment

    Inconsistent and deficient attention to relevant cues

2. ***Hostile attributional bias***

    Tendency to attribute hostile intent to others under ambiguous conditions

    Poor skill at recognizing others' benign intentions

    Poor skill at recognizing others' emotional states

    Poor skill at recognizing and labeling one's own emotional states

3. ***Emotional dysregulation***

    Frequent experience of fear and threat

    Excessive sympathetic nervous system activation following experience of threat

    Excessive testosterone release following experience of threat

    Frequent mobilization of stress response system

    Frequent disorganization across systems

    Generation of goals of self-defense, revenge, retaliation

4. ***Aggressive response generation***

    Impulsive association of social cues with reactive aggression responses

    Generation of aggressive behaviors as solutions to social problems

    Skill deficiencies in solving social problems competently

Figure 8 Summary of psychological components of defensive mindset, organized according to a social information processing model.

5. *Aggressive response evaluation and decision making*

    Impulsive tendency to implement first behavioral response called to mind

    Over valuation of self defense, revenge, retaliation, and harm

    Evaluation of aggression as leading to positive instrumental consequences

    Evaluation of aggression as leading to positive social consequences

    Evaluation of aggression as leading to positive intrapersonal consequences

    Positive judgment of the morality of aggressive behavior

    Delay discounting (favoring immediate outcomes over long-term outcomes)

6. *Inability to enact self-regulated behaviors*

    Poor verbal and motor skills for competent behavior

    High skill at aggressing

    Poor delay of gratification (overriding slow response with impulsive behaviors

Figure 8 (cont.)

The answer may be simple: *Everyone gives up.*

One of the processes in this cascade from early defensive mindset and trivial childhood misbehavior to adolescent externalizing psychopathology is that the interpersonal conflicts between children and others become so stressful that every-one gives up.

The following case illustrates this unfortunate cascade:

> *Tony (not his real name) was a first-grader in the Fast Track intervention study. Tony's single mother had very modest financial means and little support in her challenging task of rearing Tony. Although he was intelligent, he was a handful and they fought often. Tony also fought at school with peers and teachers. The Fast Track intervention staff tried valiantly to reach him, but he was resistant. Tony's mother was called to school often for meetings that she interpreted as blaming her for Tony's troubles. For a while, Tony's mother tried to impose stricter rules, but mother and son ended up fighting even more. By age 13, Tony's mother was exhausted and began to give up. She made fewer rules, looked the other way when he came home late, and ignored the school's requests to meet. Her alcoholism returned, and she actually seemed calmer in her oblivion. Unfortunately, Tony accelerated his misbehavior, quit going to school, and eventually got arrested for helping older drug dealers pass brown paper bags filled with some illicit substance from a dealer on one street corner to a buyer across the street. Sadly, Tony's mother died several years later of alcoholism; she had indeed given up.*

Pettit et al. (1999) observed this phenomenon with children in the CDP sample. During Grade 6 (age 12), parents and children were interviewed about parental monitoring and supervision, particularly parents' awareness of their children's activities and companions, their beliefs about the difficulty of tracking their children's whereabouts, and their judgments of the extent to which other adults would be available to provide supervision when their children were away at friends' homes. They interviewed children about their after-school whereabouts and activities, and they interviewed teachers in Grades 6 and 7 (ages 12 and 13) about the child's externalizing behavior problems. Not surprisingly, children who had high levels of behavior problems at age 12 were hard to monitor by their parents, who reported more difficulty in tracking their children and reduced levels of supervision. Pettit et al. also observed the reciprocal effect: Even controlling for levels of initial externalizing behavior problems, low levels of monitoring and lack of supervision by parents at age 12 predicted increases in the child's behavior problems at age 13. This is Patterson's vortex.

These patterns held among all subgroups of children studied, but they were especially strong among families living in unsafe neighborhoods, perhaps because the stakes are higher and the consequences of failing at supervision are especially potent. The patterns were also especially strong among the group of children who were initially "marginally deviant," defined as between 0 and 1 standard deviation above the mean in aggressive behavior. Caprara et al. (2007) describe how marginal deviations can grow into serious aggression. The parents of these children seemingly gave up the challenging tasks of monitoring and supervision when adolescence came along, and the child's marginally deviant behavior began to run amok.

When floodgates open, problems become more serious and spread to other bad outcomes. In the CDP, children with a defensive mindset were less likely than others to graduate from high school and to earn a college degree (Dodge et al., 2022). When they had romantic relationships, those relationships often included violent behavior by them toward their partner and by their partner toward them (e.g., shouting, pushing, hitting, punching, slapping; Fite et al., 2008). Lansford et al. (2017) found a similar pattern in the PAC study. Children displaying hostile attributional bias and aggressive problem solving during childhood are relatively likely to develop externalizing behavior psychopathology in adolescence, and this relation holds in many cultures.

What seems to happen is that as parents try to bring their defensive-minded child back into normative behavior during early adolescence, if they fail, they begin to give up on their child; in turn, these children give up on themselves and their life chances. They become cynical about their world.

4.2 Defensive Mindset Leads to Adult Dysfunction

By the time defensive children become young adults, their lives often become tragically filled with widespread dysfunction. The CDP followed children from age 4 through age 24, and Fast Track followed children from age 5 through age 32. These studies show clearly that the risk of maladaptive adult outcomes increases with increasing defensive mindedness in childhood. Of course, these predictions are probabilistic; not every defensive-minded child suffers horrible adult outcomes. Some do well, and we must learn how they turned things around.

In the CDP, Dodge et al. (2022) combined measures of deviant social information processing (hypervigilance, hostile attributional bias, aggressive response generation, and positive evaluation of reactive aggression) into an overall latent construct score for defensive mindset. We were able to locate 78% of 585 children at age 34 to test the prediction of adult outcomes. Those persons who had had high defensive mindset scores as children were more likely than others as adults to be incarcerated for violent crimes, spend more days in incarceration, and be diagnosed with externalizing psychopathology through structured interviews. Figure 9 shows that children in the highest quartile of defensive mindset scores were more than twice as likely as the children in the lowest quartile of defensive mindset scores to have been incarcerated by the time they reach 34 years of age.

Defensive-minded children also grew up to have greater rates of internalizing psychopathology (e.g., anxiety, depression). They were less likely to graduate from high school or complete college. They had lower current annual income, paid less taxes, and were more likely to be a financial burden to society through welfare. They were less likely to be married, and they reported more instances of being victimized by other adults. They were more likely to be obese and to be taking painkiller medications. As a group, they were dysfunctional in almost every realm assessed (Dodge et al., 2022).

For replication, we tested the same models with the Fast Track sample. We were able to track down 83% of children at age 32. Consistent with the CDP study, as shown in Figure 9, compared with children in the lowest quartile of defensive mindset scores, children in the highest quartile of defensive mindset scores were more than twice as likely to have been incarcerated, spent more

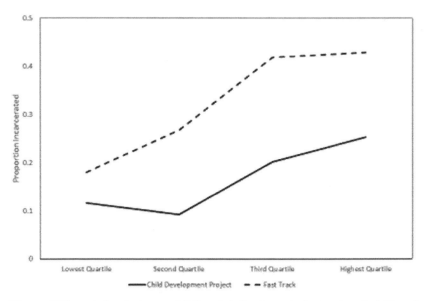

Figure 9 The relation between childhood defensive mindset and probability of adult incarceration (adapted from Dodge et al., 2022).

days incarcerated, were more likely to be diagnosed with externalizing psychopathology, were less likely to graduate from high school or complete college, had lower current annual income, paid less taxes, were more likely to be a financial burden to society, were less likely to be married, were more likely to have been victimized as an adult, and were less likely to have a close friend (Dodge et al., 2022).

4.3 Defensive Mindset Leads to Premature Mortality

Growing up with a defensive mindset must be stressful. These children are constantly vigilant and always on guard. They repeatedly get into conflicts with others. They have a hard time making financial ends meet and sustaining relationships. Their stress response systems are working overtime. Their cardiovascular system is in overdrive, with heightened heart rate and repeated large fluctuations in sympathetic nervous system responding. What toll might this mindset take on health outcomes when these children grow up?

I was part of a team (Barefoot et al., 1989) that followed samples of young adults who had taken the Minnesota Multiphasic Personality Inventory (MMPI; Schiele et al., 1943) as a part of their law schooling in 1956. The MMPI asks the respondent to say true or false to each of 567 items about themselves. Embedded in this inventory are items about defensive mindset that make up the Cook-Medley

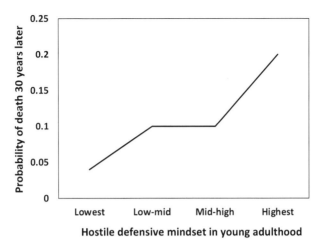

Figure 10 The relation between defensive mindset during school and later premature mortality (adapted from Barefoot et al., 1989).

Hostility Scale. These items capture several steps of defensive social information processing, including cynicism, hostile attributions, hostile affect, aggressive responding, and social avoidance. We matched their responses to publicly available death records 30 years later in 1985, which showed that about 12% of the sample had died. The higher a student's defensive mindset (Hostility Scale) score in 1956, the greater the probability that the person had died by age 50. Figure 10 shows that students in the highest quartile of defensive mindset scores were more than five times as likely as students in the lowest quartile of scores to have died prematurely 30 years later (21% versus 4%).

Barefoot et al. (1983) replicated this phenomenon with student-physicians who had been assessed for defensive mindset in the 1950s and followed through 1980. The students with defensive mindedness scores in the top half were more than six times as likely to die as the students with scores in the bottom half. Shekelle et al. (1983) assessed defensive mindset in Western Electric workers and followed them for 20 years, again showing prediction of all-cause mortality from high defensive mindset scores. Some studies have not found a significant relation between early defensive mindset scores and later mortality (e.g., McCranie et al., 1986), so the field needs to sort out why this relation holds for some populations and not others.

How do adults with defensive mindset die prematurely? Most deaths are from coronary heart disease or heart failure, and others are due to automobile accidents or interpersonal violence. Hyper-defensiveness can lead to a reckless life, out-of-control stress physiology, and tragic premature death.

5 Early Threatening Experiences Lead to Defensive Mindset

Having established that once a defensive mindset is acquired, it can have lifelong devastating consequences, what instigates the initial development of a defensive mindset? Could it be inborn, inherent, or genetic? Although some mental processes that are correlated with a defensive mindset, such as intelligence and impulsivity, may have genetic correlates, the search for a genetic origin of a defensive mindset has been futile. The processes of defensive mindset are certainly biological, but the origins are decidedly experiential. Also, with exceptions for devastating traumatic experiences that may occur later in life, such as war, physical assault, and rape, the experiences that ignite a defensive mindset typically occur early, during the first five years of life. Research on the antecedents of defensive mindset has focused on a child's experiences of physical maltreatment by parents and peer social rejection.

5.1 Physical Maltreatment

5.1.1 Physical Maltreatment Leads to Defensive Mindset

The strongest findings for the antecedents of defensive mindset come from research on children who had experienced physical abuse in the first years of life.

> "*Daryl (not his real name) was a 12-year-old child who told an interviewer about his nightly life at home when he was younger. He and his sister would wait in their shared bedroom for their father to come home in the evening. The boy was never sure whether or not it would be a night of physical beatings with a strap, or a night of being ignored, until his father walked through the door. He learned to look for cues, such as the smell of alcohol on his father's breath, irritation in his father's voice, and anger in his father's facial expressions. His father would call him into the kitchen to ask if he had completed his daily chores while his mother watched helplessly. On some evenings, the conversation would escalate to yelling and, eventually, a beating. The boy became quite skilled at detecting the signals of an impending beating and found it most adaptive to anticipate the worst.*"

Pollak and Kistler (2002) hypothesized that early experiences of child abuse would lead children to become hypervigilant to anger cues in facial expressions. They created novel stimuli using morphed images of faces depicting emotions of "happy," "sad," "fearful," and "anger," paired emotions, and morphed the faces across each of 10 computer-generated images so that a clearly angry face gradually morphed into an ambiguous expression and then into a fearful face (or a sad face or a happy face). They presented the morphing images to abused children who had been identified through the child welfare system, as well as matched non-abused children, and asked them to identify each new facial expression as quickly as they could. Children who had experienced physical abuse overidentified morphed faces as depicting anger.

> *"We view the effects observed in the present study as reflecting an adaptive process for maltreated children, allowing them to better track emotional cues of anger in the environment. The cost of such a process may be, unfortunately, to over-interpret signals as threatening and perhaps make incorrect judgments about other facial expressions"* (Pollak & Kistler, 2002, p. 9075).

In a series of studies, Pollak and Cicchetti showed that children exposed to physical abuse come to display an array of defensively oriented patterns of social information processing. Abused children show enhanced perceptual processing as indexed by an early- to mid-latency event-related potential (ERP) component (P260) while watching angry faces (Curtis & Cicchetti, 2011) and heightened P3b ERP in response to angry faces compared to other emotions (Pollak et al., 1997). Abused children quickly identify angry facial expressions with less perceptual information (Pollak & Sinha, 2002) and fewer expressive cues (Pollak et al., 2009), and they allocate more attention to vocal expressions of anger (Shackman & Pollak, 2005). Hosseini-Kamkar et al. (2023) showed through meta-analysis of 83 functional magnetic resonance imaging (fMRI) studies of 5,242 participants that exposure to adverse life experiences, including maltreatment, is reliably associated with higher amygdala reactivity and lower prefrontal cortical reactivity across a range of task domains, suggesting how early abuse might have an enduring impact on future behavior. Keil and Price (2009) assessed hostile attributional bias through hypothetical provocation scenarios in abused children identified through the child welfare system and matched non-abused children. The abused group responded with higher levels of hostile attributional bias.

Most studies of abused children identify them through the child protective services (CPS) division of county or state governments. The advantage of this sampling method is assurance that an independent professional (almost always, a social worker) has investigated and verified the fact of physical abuse or neglect. The disadvantages, however, are that this might be a select group of abused children who have come to the attention of officials because of racial bias, particularly egregious abusive behavior, or capriciousness of reporters; if so, these children might not represent the population of abused children. Also, it is plausible that the experience of being "processed" in the child welfare system has its own deleterious effects (e.g., separation from supportive family members, change of schools, blame for having been reported) that are at least partially responsible for children's later outcomes.

Our CDP research team adopted a complementary approach by sampling a community-representative group of 4-year-old children from three communities (Nashville, TN; Knoxville, TN; Bloomington, IN) and conducting interviews to identify children who had been abused in the past but had not necessarily come to the attention of public officials. We conducted conversational, open-ended, interviews with mothers and fathers privately about past experiences the children had. We were careful to warn parents that if they revealed current abuse by themselves or their partner, we would be obliged to report the exchange to the local CPS division. Nonetheless, we did hear about several cases of current possible maltreatment (usually, a mother wanting to report the behavior of her partner) and followed through with reporting. Most cases, however, were in the past and did not qualify as reportable events according to ethical self-scrutiny, local CPS authorities, and the prevailing law at the time (NB: laws vary across states and many have changed since 1986).

Trained CDP interviewers reliably coded children as having been maltreated or not. Altogether, 11.9% of the sample (69 out of 585) met criteria as having been abused in the first 5 years of life, a high figure but one that is probably an underestimate of the true experiences of children in the United States (Dodge et al., 2022). Independent interviewers assessed social information processing patterns in these children as they made their way through school, at ages 5, 6, 7, 8, 13, and 16, and created an overall defensive mindset latent score across measures and ages. The third and fourth columns of Figure 11 show the mean

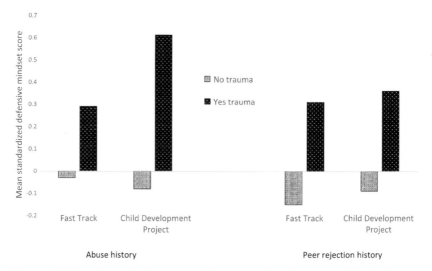

Figure 11 The effect of early physical abuse and chronic peer social rejection on the development of defensive mindset (adapted from Dodge et al., 2022.)

standardized defensive mindset construct score for the maltreated group was two-thirds of a standard deviation higher than the mean score for the non-maltreated group.

We then replicated the entire set of analyses with the Fast Track sample (Dodge et al., 2022). History of maltreatment was assessed through parent interviews at age 5, and 12.8% of the sample met criteria as having been abused. Social information processing patterns were assessed at ages 6, 7, 8, 9, 10, 11, and 14, to create a robust latent score for defensive mindedness. Replicating the CDP, one can see in the left-most columns of Figure 11 that the maltreated group had a defensive mindset score that was one-third of a standard deviation larger than the mean for the non-maltreated group. Maltreated children are more likely than others to develop defensive mindset with a replicated effect size somewhere between one- and two-thirds standard deviations.

5.1.2 Abused Children Grown up

What happens to abused children as they grow up? A committee of the National Research Council (Petersen et al., 2014) adopted the terminology of "cascading effects" to describe how the early experience of physical maltreatment has an enduring effect on children's social cognition, which cascades into long-term effects on children's maladaptation to school, peers, and, eventually, the adult world.

Our team (Dodge et al., 1990; Weiss et al., 1992) followed the 4-year-old boys and girls of the CDP and Fast Track across childhood to track outcomes for abused children. We took into account prior factors (including socioeconomic status, single parent household, child temperament, and family ecology) that might be correlated with outcomes in order to isolate the effect of maltreatment. At the first time point at age 5, direct observers found that abused children (relative to non-abused peers) displayed more frequent aggressive behaviors toward peers on the playground, teachers rated them as more aggressive, and peers rated them as more aggressive. In late adolescence, Lansford et al. (2007) gathered court records and interviews to find that 34% of abused children had been arrested, in contrast with just 20% of non-abused children, with higher rates of arrest for both violent crimes and nonviolent crimes. At age 21, structured interviews indicated that the abused group was much more likely to have engaged in violence in their romantic relationships (both as perpetrator and as victim; Pettit et al., 2010), serious violent delinquency (e.g., physical assault, use of weapon, sexual assault, gang fight), and to have been fired from a job (Lansford et al., 2007). Only 14% of the abused group graduated from college, in contrast with 30% of the non-abused group. By age 24, among girls, the abused group was more likely than the non-abused group to engage in substance abuse, and, among boys, the abused group was more likely than the non-abused group to engage in violent crime (Lansford et al., 2010).

By age 26, the life course outcomes for the formerly abused children looked grim. At this age, Lansford et al. (2021) relied on self-report and administrative records and interviewed a peer or partner to get a fresh objective perspective. Only 53% of the abused children had become employed full time, in contrast with 69% of the non-abused group; and 20% of the abused group was receiving public assistance, in contrast with 10% for the non-abused group. The abused group had worse overall health and more frequent risky sexual behaviors. They were twice as likely to have been convicted of a crime in the past 12 months. Diagnosed psychopathology among the abused group continued to be high, with higher rates (compared with the non-abused group) of disorders for antisocial personality, attention deficit hyperactivity, and anxiety. As adults at ages 32–34, the outcomes had not gotten any better (Dodge et al., 2022). The formerly abused group was more likely than the non-abused group to have been incarcerated and for longer periods, less likely to have graduated from college, less likely to be employed, less likely to be married, more likely to be on government assistance, and more likely to have been victimized by others.

The replicated findings are clear. Children who had experienced physical abuse in early life are at higher risk than others to engage in violent behavior and to experience a diverse array of tragic outcomes including substance abuse, failure in establishing and keeping social relationships, and dependency on government and others. Not all abused children drifted into lives of violent crime; some never became aggressive but instead failed to get "on track" in school, employment, and life. Early abuse derailed them, disorganized their relationships, and debilitated them. These associations are probabilistic. Not all abused children have poor outcomes, so the search for mediators and moderators is crucial in the quest for preventive intervention.

5.1.3 Defensive Mindset Mediates the Effect of Maltreatment on Adult Outcomes

How does early childhood maltreatment wreak such awful lifelong outcomes? The development of a defensive mindset, depicted in Figure 12, may be a major mediating process to account for how early adversity leads to long-term dysfunction.

To demonstrate mediation statistically, Baron and Kenny (1986) proposed that four empirical conditions must be met. First, the initial driver (here, the

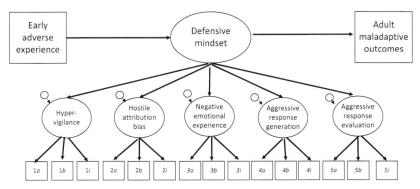

Figure 12 A model of how early adverse experience leads to maladaptive outcomes through the acquisition of a defensive mindset.

experience of physical abuse as rated by a trained interviewer of mothers and fathers at child age 4) must predict the hypothesized outcome (here, children's frequency of aggressive behavior at age 5 as measured by direct observations, peer nomination, and teacher ratings). Second, the driver must predict the hypothesized mediator (here, defensive processing measured by hypervigilance to threat, hostile attributional bias, retaliatory response generation, and positive evaluation of retaliation). Third, the mediator must predict the outcome. Fourth, in a regression model, the magnitude of the relation between the driver and the outcome must be reduced when the mediator is entered into the model.

In 1990, the CDP team (Dodge et al., 1990) hypothesized that the experience of physical abuse in the first 5 years of life would drive children to become aggressive toward their peers and the effect would be mediated through the development of defensive patterns of social information processing. All measured processing steps were empirically supported as mediators.

What about the long-term? The CDP team continued to test whether childhood defensive mindset mediates the effect of early abuse on children's maladaptive outcomes as they get older. Dodge et al. (1995) found that defensive processing partially mediates the effect of early abuse on aggression in later elementary school. Dodge et al. (2022) found that a comprehensive and highly reliable construct measure of defensive mindset as assessed during childhood partially mediates the effect of early abuse on a range of dysfunctional outcomes at age 33, including a large number of days being incarcerated, a high rate of externalizing psychopathology, low current income, a low level of ultimate education, being victimized by others in adulthood, and not being married. These mediational tests for all of the same outcomes were replicated with participants in the Fast Track project at age 32 (Dodge et al., 2022). Although these tests show replicated and robust mediational processes, it must be noted that the magnitude of mediation was modest. Typically, about a quarter of the variance in adult outcomes was accounted for by defensive mindedness, indicating that other processes must also be involved.

5.2 Harsh and Insensitive Parenting

It does not take the extreme experience of physical abuse for children to develop a defensive mindset. Parents shape their child's development in many other ways, through modeling of behaviors, reinforcement and punishment in the course of discipline, and their attachment relationship with their child. Cassidy et al. (1996) hypothesized that secure attachment of an infant to the mother could protect the child from developing a defensive mindset. She assessed attachment security in families and later presented hypothetical provocation scenarios to children. Securely attached children were more likely than others to identify benign intention in others, whereas children who had been rejected by parents demonstrated greater frequency of hostile attributional bias. McElwain and colleagues (2008) replicated these findings using the sample of 1,071 children in the NICHD childcare study. They assessed the mother–infant attachment relationship in the first 36 months of life, followed children into school at age 6, and assessed children's hostile attributional biases in response to hypothetical provocation stories. Children who had been insecurely attached to mothers in early life were more likely to display hostile attributional biases toward classmates. Zajac et al. (2020) found a similar pattern in their longitudinal study: Insecurely attached infants were more likely to demonstrate hostile attributional biases by the time they turned 8 years old. This team found a particular type of insecure attachment, disorganized attachment, was most strongly predictive of latter hostile attributional biases.

Coe et al. (2020) found that other parenting styles can lay the foundation for children's defensive mindset. Based on family systems theory, they videorecorded parents interacting with their preschool-aged children, meticulously coded behaviors, and observed that "detouring" (a pattern of two parents conspiring against their child in blaming the child, excluding the child, or the like) predicted children's development of hostile attributional biases toward peers in first grade. Yaros et al. (2016) found that parents who engage in physical aggression and use corporal punishment with their children (short of legally defined maltreatment) have children who, in turn, are relatively likely to display hostile attributional biases.

Lansford et al., (2010) provide the most global empirical test of relations among parenting behavior, children's social information processing, and children's externalizing psychopathology. At child age 8, parents reported on their use of corporal punishment and rejection of their child. When children were 10 years old, they responded to questions about hypothetical social provocations to assess hostile attributional bias. When children were 12 years old, their externalizing behavior problems were assessed. Multigroup structural equation models revealed that parents' early rejection and corporal punishment of their children predicted children's likelihood of developing hostile attributional biases, which, in turn, predicted children's later externalizing problems, and children's hostile attributional biases mediated a significant portion of the effect of parenting on children's psychopathology.

5.3 Traumatic Peer Relationships

Peers exert extreme power in shaping a child's sense of self-worth, anxiety, and attitudes toward school. Peers can be cruel or inviting, teasing or comforting. Some children are chronically excluded from play, called names, or laughed at, merely because of a physical disability, the clothes they wear, the fact they live on the wrong side of the tracks, or for no reason at all. Children's early experiences of chronic social rejection or victimization by peers can have a strong influence on children's development of a defensive mindset. A common way to measure peer relationships is through sociometric interviews in which all peers in a classroom are asked to nominate children whom they like the most and like the least, with responses being summed to yield scores for "liked most," "liked least," and "social preference" (the difference between liked most and liked least). Peers can also nominate children who are most frequently victimized. MacKinnon-Lewis et al. (1999) found that early low acceptance by peers predicted children's later beliefs that peers will be unfriendly. Egan et al. (1998) found that early victimization by peers predicted later feelings of ineffectiveness and that no action by children would or could lead to successful outcomes with peers.

We (Dodge et al., 2022) followed the children of the CDP from childhood into adulthood and found empirical support for each of the four components in this model with regard to traumatic peer relationships. First, chronic peer social rejection in childhood is associated with many problems in adulthood. Second, as shown in Figure 10, chronic peer social rejection predicts the likelihood that children will develop a defensive mindset. Third, the child with a defensive mindset is likely to grow into adulthood experiencing an array of maladjustment outcomes. Finally, the development of a defensive mindset mediates the effect of early peer rejection on many of these problem outcomes, including being incarcerated, demonstrating externalizing psychopathology, failing to get a college degree, having low income, being victimized by others in adulthood, and failing to get or stay married. Most of these findings were replicated in the Fast Track sample (Dodge et al., 2022). A defensive mindset appears to be a major psychological process through which early adverse child experiences lead to long-term dysfunction.

6 Clinical Intervention

After the ill-fated role-taking training experiment was a success at demonstrating the intervention was a failure, I spent a decade working with students and colleagues to identify six factors that empirical studies show they decrease the likelihood aggressive children will make a hostile attribution about a peer's intention.

1. *De-personalize the peer's behavior.* Dodge and Frame (1982) presented aggressive and nonaggressive children with hypothetical provocations and experimentally manipulated the target of a peer's provocation as either the self (that is, the subject) or a third-party peer. That is, children were asked to imagine a peer provoked them or another peer. When the target was the self, aggressive children were 39% more likely than nonaggressive children to attribute hostile intent, but when the target was another peer, aggressive and nonaggressive children were virtually identical in their attributions. Dodge and Frame speculated that intervention might teach aggressive children to de-personalize their encounters and to decrease the high emotional valence of their experiences.

2. *Relax before responding.* Dodge and Somberg (1987) asked aggressive and nonaggressive children to attribute intentions to hypothetical provocations by a peer directed toward the self under experimentally manipulated conditions in which they first asked the children either to relax or to consider past threats. Under conditions of recalling past threats, the aggressive children were more likely than nonaggressive children to attribute hostile intent, but this difference virtually disappeared when children were induced to relax before responding to the provocation. Intervention might be directed toward teaching aggressive children to relax before responding to conflict situations.

3. *Slow down before responding.* Dodge and Newman (1981) asked aggressive and nonaggressive boys to participate in a detective game in which the task was to accumulate evidence in order to decide whether or not a peer had acted with benevolent or hostile intent. Aggressive boys responded more quickly and made their decisions with less information than nonaggressive boys. Aggressive boys also over-attributed hostile intent to peers, but only when they responded

quickly. The findings suggest that training aggressive boys to slow down before responding could lead to fewer biased attributions on their part.

4. *Attend to all cues before responding.* In the experiment by Dodge and Frame (1982), the investigators found that aggressive children made hostile attributions primarily when they failed to attend to all the relevant cues that had been presented. When they attended to all cues, aggressive children's attributions were similar to those of nonaggressive children, suggesting that intervention should teach aggressive children to attend to all pertinent cues before responding.

5. *Utilize actual cues rather than self-schemas when making an attribution.* Dodge and Tomlin (1987) asked aggressive and nonaggressive boys and girls to play a game with multiple trials in which they were to imagine being provoked by a peer. For each trial, they were given eight "testimonies" of clues about the peer's behavior and were asked to make an interpretation of the peer's intention, to explain the basis for their interpretation, and to recall the clues. The investigators experimentally manipulated the set of cues across trials, such that the weight of the clues supported either a hostile intention or a benign intention. Relative to non-aggressive children, aggressive children were less likely to cite actually presented clues and less likely to recall benign clues; instead, they were more likely to cite their own past experiences and self-schemas. The aggressive children's pattern of relying on self-schemas rather than currently presented information was associated with their relative inaccuracy at interpreting others' intentions, suggesting that intervention might be directed to helping aggressive children utilize information in their current social world rather than rely on preexisting stereotypes and schemas.

6. *Others should make intention information clear.* This last factor is not a directive to aggressive children but rather to others in their environment. Dodge et al. (1984) presented children with videorecorded scenarios in which the cues indicating the intention of a peer provocateur varied experimentally to be more or less clear. As cues became clearer, socially rejected – aggressive children became more accurate and less biased toward interpreting hostile intentions. The investigators speculated that intervention environments could emphasize being very clear with aggressive children about the intentions of a peer or authority figure, to minimize bias and inaccuracy.

The sum of these studies and clinical experiences suggest a strategy for intervention with aggressive children that would focus on helping them respond to social conflicts with slower, more intentional, and more mindful processes that attend to the current situation. What remained was to find a clinical context in which to develop and test an intervention based on a decade of empirical science.

6.1 Fast Track

In 1989, the nation witnessed a growing youth violence rate and public outcry to bring back order. The National Institute of Mental Health responded by allocating extra funds and calling for studies to test novel intervention approaches to prevent young children from growing into chronically violent predators. To meet the challenge, Coie organized a team including myself, Greenberg, Bierman, Lochman, and McMahon to bring together state-of-the-science knowledge to create a comprehensive multi-year intervention for highly aggressive six-year-old children who were on their way to chronic violence and to test impact of the novel intervention on adolescent violence outcomes through a randomized controlled trial. This team turned into a 30-year collaboration testing the Fast Track intervention. In later years, the team added Pinderhughes, Crowley, Lansford, and Godwin. In the following section, I provide my perspective on the Fast Track design and interpretation of findings. Each team member undoubtedly had his or her own lens through which to view Fast Track. I view changing defensive mindset as the primary focus and primary mediator of long-term intervention benefits.

6.1.1 The Fast Track Intervention Components

The Fast Track intervention is described in detail in a volume by the Conduct Problems Prevention Research Group (2019). During planning, the Fast Track team addressed two questions: 1) what do we want aggressive children to learn? and 2) through what modalities could we accomplish that learning?

1. *What do we want aggressive children to learn?* Based on the body of research and clinical experience, we know a crucial goal of intervention with highly aggressive six-year-old children must be to teach them to slow down and to apply executive control over their emotional reactions before they respond with impulsive aggression. How could we teach slow processing? The team adapted a metaphor from Weissberg, the stop light, and its three steps of Stop, Think, and Go, as depicted in Figure 13, and developed a curriculum around that metaphor. The curriculum was implemented by bachelor-level trained Educational Coordinators (ECs).

The first part of the curriculum is to help children learn that when they encounter a problem, any kind of problem, they should first STOP, slow down, and calm down. ECs played games and role-played stories to teach children what a "problem" is; that is, a problem is any time they feel unhappy, stuck, hurt by someone else, or in trouble, or any time someone else seems to have a problem with them. ECs helped aggressive children identify strategies for slowing down, such as counting to ten, taking a deep breath, feeling their heart beat more slowly, and looking away. They played games to help the children practice, they observed them in free play with peers, and they seized

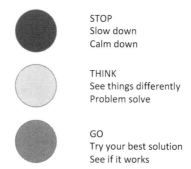

STOP
Slow down
Calm down

THINK
See things differently
Problem solve

GO
Try your best solution
See if it works

Figure 13 The stop light metaphor to teach self-control and problem solving (adapted from Weissberg et al., 1990).

on naturally occurring problem events to practice slowing down. Although there are many components to competent social information processing that would take many years to master, ECs declared a success if during the first year aggressive children could simply slow down.

Once ECs got children to slow down, they directed them to go to the yellow light (depicted in the figure in gray shade), where they were encouraged children to engage in other mental processes, starting with recognizing one's own and others' emotions. They began to teach children to "see things differently," that is, to consider multiple divergent interpretations of their problem. Here is where hostile attributional biases come front and center: Could it be that the other child did not see you before he ran into you? Might it be that the teacher was not trying to make fun of you but was simply trying to get all children to be quiet?

As children learned to consider multiple interpretations of their situation and to understand (and regulate) their emotions, ECs encouraged them to begin a problem-solving process. What might they be able to do if that particular problem occurred to them? ECs encouraged expansive thinking to get children out of their old habits. They taught them the difference between thinking about what they could do and actually doing it – impulse control. They taught children to consider more than one way of reacting before deciding to react. And they taught children to make the decision they believe is best for them.

When children learned the process of making a behavioral decision, ECs taught them to go to the green light (depicted in the figure as dark gray) to try it out. The process does not end there. While at the green light, ECs taught children to observe themselves and others. Did that decision solve their problem? Are they calmer and happier? Have others stopped bothering them? If not, they would teach them to start over by going back to the red light.

2. *Through what modalities can we intervene to help aggressive children?* The intervention team was realistic enough to realize that helping aggressive

children become less defensive minded would require a multi-pronged, all-out effort over a long time. It had taken years for children to develop a defensive mindset; it would take years to change it. The team committed to intervening with these children for 10 years, through high school. The intervention began in first grade (age 6) on a weekly basis, moved to biweekly sessions the next year, and monthly sessions thereafter. The components were as follows:

Friendship Groups. Children were invited to attend Friendship Groups of four to eight children held after school or on weekends that targeted children's social-cognitive skills of accurate awareness of others' intentions, emotional expression and emotional understanding, emotion regulation, anger control, and social problem-solving skills. EC leaders were assisted by para-professionals to use role-playing, videotaping, and coaching methods that included direct instruction and modeling to build skill concepts, behavioral rehearsal, practice, and feedback. As the children moved into middle school (ages 11–14), group sessions populated only by high-risk children were discontinued because of the emerging literature on the dangers of deviant peer influence that could occur in volatile peer groups and replaced them with mentoring sessions and individual planning meetings between the EC and the children.

PATHS®. Classroom teachers taught a grade-level version of the PATHS® (Promoting Alternative Thinking Strategies) Curriculum (Greenberg et al., 2011), 2–3 times per week in Grades 1 to 5 (ages 6–10) to all classmates of aggressive children. This curriculum reinforced skills taught in the Friendship Groups and brought the skills to the entire peer group. The curriculum targeted prosocial skills (helping, sharing, cooperating), self-control, emotional awareness and understanding, and social problem solving.

Peer pairing. Prior research had suggested that including classmates in social skills training plans could give aggressive children a chance to practice what they had learned in Friendship Groups with other children and promote positive changes in peers' behavior and attitudes toward aggressive children (Bierman & Furman, 1984). ECs provided a supervised half-hour play session with classroom peers each week.

Academic tutoring. Although social skills were the centerpiece of the Fast Track intervention, the team knew that aggressive children need help in other domains as well, so they developed a phonics-based tutoring program to teach reading skills based on work by Coie and Krehbiel (1984). Aggressive children received three tutoring sessions per week in the first year and extra tutoring in subsequent years based on need.

Parenting groups with home visits. The team knew they needed parents' support, so they delivered Parent Groups that were based on ideas by Forehand and McMahon (1981) and which were delivered while the children were attending Friendship Groups. These groups were led by Family Coordinators (FCs) who focused on improving positive parent–child interactions, reducing harsh and punitive discipline, and increasing consistent limit setting. FCs told parents that in the children's Friendship Groups, they were teaching them to slow down through the stoplight metaphor; inevitably, at least one parent would comment, "Well, we could all use that help." So the FCs incorporated the stoplight tool in teaching parents to respond to their children in more deliberate, mindful ways; this practice not only helped parents in their discipline behavior, it enabled parents to use the same language and terms that the team was teaching their children.

The team supplemented Parent Groups with individualized home visits, which provided the FCs an opportunity to understand each family's unique situation and to build a strong working alliance with each primary caregiver.

Parent–child sharing. The team followed Parent Group and Friendship Group sessions with a half-hour parent–child sharing session created by Lochman that had two goals: 1) to foster positive parent–child relationships; and 2) to provide parents a chance to practice the skills introduced in Parent Groups, with staff guidance.

Mentoring. The team added a mentoring program in the later years to provide a same-sex, same-race, community volunteer mentor for children who lacked an adult role model in their lives. Mentors were briefed in the goals of the intervention and encouraged to support the interventions, including the stop light model.

6.1.2 The Fast Track Randomized Controlled Trial

How could the team evaluate the impact of this massive intervention? We matched the complexity of the intervention with an equally complex randomized controlled trial. The intervention and the evaluation trial were implemented in each of three years in each of four communities (Durham, NC; Nashville, TN; rural central PA; and Seattle, WA), which afforded a diverse sample of children and multiple opportunities to hone and test the program. The team recruited 55 high-risk schools based on demographic characteristics about the crime and poverty rates of the neighborhoods they served. From the population of 9,594 kindergarteners in these schools, the team used a multiple-gating procedure to ask teachers (and then parents) to screen and select 891 (top 9% of total) highly aggressive children. These children were randomly assigned (based on the school cluster they attended) to receive the Fast Track intervention ($n=445$) or serve as a control ($n=446$). The targeted children were a high-risk group, mostly from backgrounds of disadvantage or trauma. Sixty-nine percent of the children were boys. Fifty percent were African American, 47% were European American, and 2% came from other groups. Fifty-eight percent lived with single parents, and 40% were in the lowest socioeconomic class. Proof of their high risk would come later when the team followed the control group into adulthood and found that, at age 26, without the Fast Track intervention, 69% ended up meeting diagnostic criteria as having a psychiatric disorder.

The team implemented the intervention with high fidelity and strong participation (CPPRG, 1999). In the first year, over 99% of the families assigned to intervention consented to participate in the intervention and received at least one session, and 72% attended more than half of each intervention component. In later years, participation declined modestly, but most families remained engaged.

To evaluate the impact of Fast Track on children, we appointed an independent research team to follow the children assigned to intervention (whether or not they actually participated) and the control children across time by interviewing children and their parents each summer and their teachers and peers each school year (for five years). We also retrieved school records and, later, criminal records. We successfully tracked 85% of the original sample into adulthood and continue to follow the original sample today as they reach their mid-30s and have children of their own.

6.1.3 The Impact of Fast Track on Aggressive Children

Impact on defensive mindset

The team's initial focus was to determine whether the intervention accomplished its proximal goal to improve children's social-cognitive skills, particularly the reduction of defensive mindset. The assessment protocol followed the social information processing model to test the effect of Fast Track on children's processing patterns. Although not every outcome yielded a statistically significant effect, in general, the intervention was successful, although it took some time. Figure 14 depicts these effects.

At the end of the first grade year (CPPRG, 1999), the children randomly assigned to receive the Fast Track intervention demonstrated more skillful and less defensive processing than control children in four of the five steps of processing that had been assessed. Intervention-assigned children performed better at recognizing emotions in others (Step 1), coping with difficult emotions (Step 3), generating less aggressive solutions in social problem solving (Step 4), and decision making in response to social problems (Step 5), with effect sizes ranging from .12 to .36 standard deviations. In the first year, the intervention did not have any effect on children's hostile attributional biases. The team

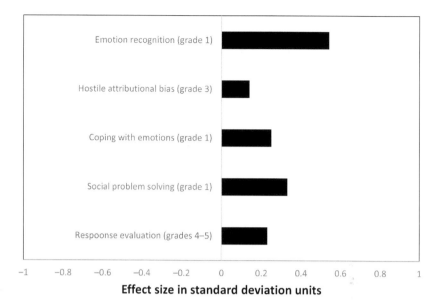

Effect size in standard deviation units

Figure 14 Summary of significant effect sizes (in standard deviations) for the positive impact of random assignment to the Fast Track intervention on five steps of defensive processing (adapted from CPPRG, 1999, 2002).

realized this central component of children's defensive mindset would take more time to break. After three years of intervention, the team found a positive impact: Fast Track-assigned children displayed lower (better) scores for hostile attributional bias than control children with a significant effect size of .14 (CPPRG, 2002). The team also found sustained positive impact of random assignment to the Fast Track intervention on reduction of components of defensive mindset and improvement of social competence in Grades 4 and 5 (ages 9 and 10) (CPPRG, 2004; Dodge et al., 2013).

Impact on aggressive behavior in elementary school

Next, the team evaluated the effect of Fast Track on children's aggressive behavior problems. Again, not all tests proved statistically significant, but, in general, the intervention was successful in reducing children's aggressive behavior and improving social adjustment and well-being across the first five years, as shown in Figure 15.

At the end of the first year, objective playground observers coded more time in positive peer interaction and fewer aggressive-and-noncompliant behaviors for the intervention-assigned children than control children, with effect sizes of .27 and .31, respectively. Peer sociometric interviews revealed that intervention-assigned

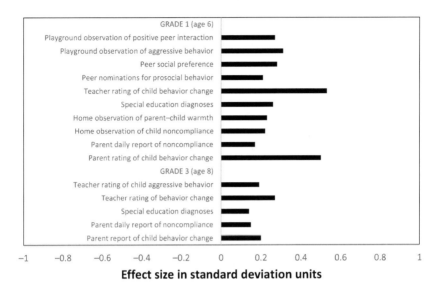

Figure 15 Summary of significant effect sizes (in standard deviations) for the positive impact of random assignment to the Fast Track intervention on children's aggressive behavior, social adjustment, and well-being during childhood (adapted from CPPRG, 1999, 2002).

children received higher social preference scores and more nominations for pro-social behavior (effect sizes = .28 and .21, respectively). Classroom teachers rated the behavior change of intervention children much more positively than for control children (effect size = .53). School records indicated fewer special education diagnoses (mostly for behavior problems) for intervention than control children (effect size = .26). At home, objective observers coded greater warmth and less noncompliance/aggression in parent–child dyads of intervention families than control families (effect sizes = .23 and .22, respectively). The Parent Daily Report (based on four days of nightly telephone calls to parents) revealed fewer instances of misbehavior for intervention children than control children (effect size = .17), and parents rated the behavior change of their intervention children more positively than did parents of control children (effect size = .50).

At the end of third grade, the pattern persisted. Classroom teachers continued to rate the aggressive behavior problems as lower and behavior change across the year as more positive for intervention than control children (effect sizes = .19 and .27, respectively). Special education diagnoses continued to be lower for intervention children (effect size = .14). At home, the Parent Daily Report revealed fewer instances of misbehavior (effect size = .15), and parents reported more positive child behavior change (effect size = .20).

Impact on antisocial behavior in adolescence

As the children moved into adolescence, we all thought disaster had struck. It seemed that the intervention children (and their classmates) had "lost their minds" and become obsessed with deviance, independence, and misbehavior. Analyses of children's skills and behaviors produced significant effects of the Fast Track intervention for only two (age 13 hyperactivity and delinquency behaviors) of the 17 variables tested (CPPRG, 2010).

When the children entered high school, however, significant positive impact of random assignment to the intervention had returned. Primary measures were the Self-Reported Delinquency (SRD) scale, as well as other measures such as diagnoses of psychiatric disorder. This instrument documents the number of times each of 25 delinquent acts, including property damage, theft, physical assault, and substance use, were committed in the past year. The intervention group had a mean delinquency score that was 26% lower than the mean score for the control group (CPPRG, 2007).

Next, we tested the primary hypothesis guiding the intervention that improvement in children's social information processing patterns would mediate an indirect impact on adolescent antisocial behavior. The model and findings are depicted in Figure 16. As hypothesized, random assignment to Fast Track had significant positive impact on reducing children's hostile attributional bias, aggressive response generation, and favorable evaluations of the consequences of aggressing.

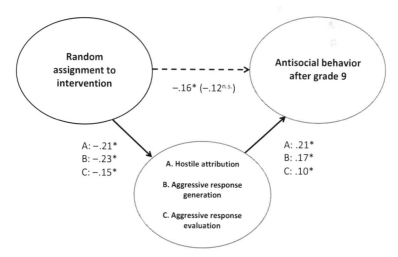

Figure 16 The Fast Track intervention targets the long-term prevention of delinquency by changing children's defensive mindset (adapted from Dodge et al., 2013). Figures represent path coefficients, with "*" indicating a significant path at p < .05.

In turn, these processing patterns predicted antisocial behavior at age 14 (after grade 9) and significantly accounted for about 25% of the effect of Fast Track on antisocial behavior (Dodge et al., 2013).

Impact on outcomes in adulthood

The Fast Track intervention continued for 10 years, through age 16. At that point, the program "graduated" children and wished them well. The research team has followed participants for another 20 years and continues following them today as participants have reached full adulthood, become employed and community citizens, and have families of their own. Intervention staff members have attended numerous weddings of "Fast Trackers," celebrated their life successes, consulted when crises ensued, and even mourned several deaths. Some participants have spent time in prison, and some have become contributing citizens. Systematic analysis indicates the overall stability of positive impacts of the early intervention on adult life outcomes across a wide array of domains, as depicted in Figure 17 for crime and social competence and in Figure 18 for health and mental health.

Impact on antisocial behavior in young adulthood

Four years after the intervention ended, at age 20, the investigators assessed antisocial behavior through three measures and found sustained impact of random

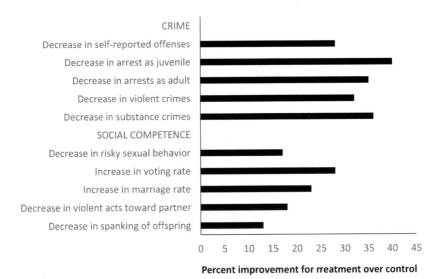

Figure 17 The impact of Fast Track on crime and social competence (adapted from CPPRG, 2015).

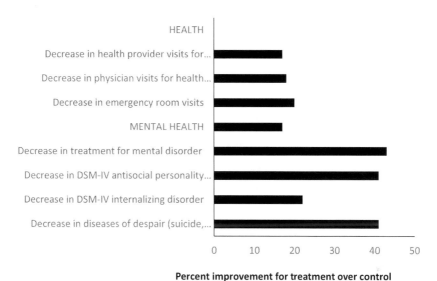

Figure 18 The impact of Fast Track on health and mental health (adapted from CPPRG, 2015).

assignment to the Fast Track intervention on all three measures. Sorenson, Dodge, and CPPRG (2016) found that, relative to the control participants, the incidence rate of cumulative self-reported delinquent offenses was 27% lower for Fast Track participants, and review of court records showed that Fast Track participants were 39% more likely to have never been arrested as a juvenile and 34% more likely to have never been arrested as an adult.

Again, the team was interested in testing the processes through which Fast Track might have achieved this positive impact. We pitted three plausible processes against each other, all of which were focal targets of the Fast Track intervention and measured during the first five years of intervention. Latent constructs were created for each of three potential mediating processes: (1) nondefensive social-information-processing patterns (indicated by strong emotion recognition, lack of hostile attributional bias, competent emotion coping, nonaggressive response generation, and evaluation of aggression as leading to non-desirable conse-quences); (2) interpersonal behavioral competence (indicated by high peer social preference, high peer-nominated prosocial behavior, high teacher-rated social competence, high teacher-rated authority acceptance, and low aggression prob-lems); and (3) cognitive and academic competence (indicated by high language arts grades, high reading test score, and high teacher-rated academic competence). Random assignment to Fast Track had produced positive impacts during the first five years on all three of these constructs, so it was plausible that any of them could account for impact on young-adult antisocial behavior. We tested mediation through two different approaches, structural equation modeling and reduced-form modeling (used in economics). The two approaches yielded similar findings. First, although Fast Track had improved the academic competence factor, it played no role in mediating any antisocial outcome. Second, both the interpersonal behavioral competence and nondefensive social information processing factors mediated part of the effect of Fast Track on antisocial outcomes. Third, the intervention's effect on nondefensive processing accounted for most of the mediating effects, up to 68% of Fast Track's effect on reducing antisocial crime at age 20. The primary proximal target for childhood intervention to prevent serious antisocial behavior outcomes in adulthood should be the reduction of a defensive mindset.

Impact on violent crime and psychiatric disorder

At age 26, the investigators once again conducted a round of clinical interviews with participants. We also interviewed an adult peer of each participant, such as a friend, coworker, or spouse, to get a more objective, third-party perspective, and averaged self and peer reports. By this age, the effects of Fast Track had become larger and had spread to multiple domains of life (CPPRG, 2015). Random assignment to Fast Track at age 5 reduced the number and severity of violent crimes ever committed by participants through age 26 by 31%, substance crimes by 35%, DSM-IV diagnoses of antisocial personality by 41%, DSM-IV diagnoses of internalizing avoidant personality by 22%, and risky sexual behaviors by 18%. Combining across any DSM-IV externalizing, internalizing, or substance use disorder, 69% of all control group participants received a psychiatric diagnosis, in contrast with 59% for the intervention group. This difference was a modest effect but has huge implications for financial benefits and well-being.

Because we had found significant effects of Fast Track on internalizing outcomes even though the target of intervention had been externalizing outcomes, the team wanted to examine them more closely. Godwin and CPPRG (2020) found that random assignment to Fast Track reduced so-called "diseases of despair" (which included suicidal ideation, suicidal attempts, weekly hazardous drinking, and weekly opioid use) by 41%. The investigators tested the processes responsible for this effect with the three constructs we had identified earlier (academic competence, interpersonal competence, and defensive processing) and found that Fast Track's effect on interpersonal competence mediated the effect (by 20%) on diseases of despair. Fast Track's effect on academic competence and defensive processing did not mediate this internalizing outcome.

So the growing narrative had become the following. The Fast Track intervention was successful at improving each of three dimensions of aggressive children's childhood lives, defensive social information processing, interpersonal behavioral competence, and academic competence. In turn, the effect on defensive processing in childhood accounted for reverberating effects on adult violent crime. The effect on interpersonal competence accounted for effects on adult internalizing outcomes and diseases of despair. The effect on academic competence was gratifying but did not mediate any adult impact.

Impact on health and mental health service utilization

After each year of high school, the investigators interviewed participants and their parents to assess the adolescents' history of utilization of health and mental health services. By the end of high school, compared with the control group, random assignment to the Fast Track intervention was associated with 16% fewer visits to a physician for health problems, 14% fewer visits to any health services provider for health problems, 18% fewer emergency room visits, and a 43% lower likelihood of receiving treatment for a mental disorder (Jones et al., 2010).

Impact on well-being and civic engagement

As part of the age-26 clinical interview, the investigators asked participants to report about their lives. Those participants who had been assigned to Fast Track reported greater overall well-being (effect size of .12) and greater happiness in life (effect size of .19).

This greater sense of well-being spilled over into more civic engagement. Holbein (2017) examined public records of voting behavior and found that children who had been randomly assigned to Fast Track at age 5 were more likely to grow up to vote in elections as an adult than were control children (33% voters versus 26% voters). Furthermore, intervention-induced improvement in defensive mindset measured in childhood mediated about half of the effect of Fast Track on adult voting behavior. In contrast, academic competence and interpersonal competence did not mediate this impact. Defensive mindset inhibits people from voting in elections, and intervention that targets defensive mindset can improve the rate of participation in voting.

The next generation: Impact on family formation

As the participants grew into their 20s and 30s, the investigators tracked their romantic relationships, family formation, and parenting behavior. We are still in contact with 80% of the original sample. At age 26, compared with control participants, participants who had been assigned to Fast Track committed 19%

fewer violent acts against a romantic partner (CPPRG, 2015). Among those who had become parents, Fast Track-assigned participants had physically spanked or hit their child 13% less frequently than had the control group.

Analyses at age 34 focused on marriage: The children who had been randomly assigned to the Fast Track intervention at age 5 were more likely than control children to be married (rather than single or cohabitating; 27% for the intervention group versus 22% for the control group), and the intervention-assigned group had more children than did the control group (mean of 1.93 offspring versus 1.67 offspring) (Lansford et al., 2023).

Impact on enduring biological processes

The intervention ended at age 16, and it was gratifying to see that impact continued for another 16 years. We wondered whether there was a corresponding enduring effect on biological processes. The team targeted testosterone release because it is known to play a mediating role in aggressive responding in males. At age 26, Carré et al. (2014) brought participants (males living in Durham; this site was the only one equipped for this sub-study) into the laboratory and asked them to play a computer game against a (fictitious) peer with whom they competed for a monetary prize. In the middle of the game, the peer "stole" some of the participant's earnings. We measured both testosterone release during the game (through repeated saliva sample collection) and reactive aggressive behavior (measured by the participants' retaliatory theft of the peer's earnings).

The findings were striking. Random assignment to the Fast Track intervention 21 years earlier decreased participants' release of testosterone and reactive aggressive behavior following the experience of a peer's provocation. In the 10-minute period after provocation by the peer, the Fast Track participants decreased testosterone release by 6% on average, whereas the control group increased testosterone release by 7%, an effect size of .61. Furthermore, testosterone release mediated 26% of the impact of Fast Track on reactive aggression toward the peer. The Fast Track intervention had "taught" children to respond to provocation with less testosterone release, which in turn led to less reactive aggressive behavior, and this effect had gotten "under the skin" and was sustained biologically and behaviorally through age 26.

Generalizability of impact across groups

What is particularly striking about the effect of Fast Track is the consistency of its impact across the different groups of participants: The investigators observed a positive effect of Fast Track among each of the 13 sub-groups they studied: male and female; European American and African American; Cohorts 1, 2, and

3; Durham, Nashville, rural PA, and Seattle sites; and highest and moderate risk children. Figure 19 depicts the consistent impact on the most general measure in adulthood, being diagnosed with any psychiatric disorder (CPPRG, 2015).

6.1.4 Complementary Interventions to Change Defensive Mindset

It is essential to replicate findings and to see whether other investigators replicate and extend findings. Bierman et al. (2022) conducted a randomized controlled trial of the Friendship Group component of the Fast Track intervention with 224 young children and found positive impact of assignment to intervention on improving social-cognitive skills, reducing externalizing behavior reduction, and improving peer relationships.

Other investigators have tested their own interventions to address defensive mindset with diverse populations of aggressive children, with encouraging results. Hudley and Graham (1993) tested an intervention to alter the attributions made by African-American boys about peer provocations and found positive impact on reducing peer-directed aggressive behavior. Fraser and colleagues (2005) created and tested the Making Choices: Social Problems Solving Skills for Children (MC) program with 8-year-old children and found that the program improves children's social information-processing skills and reduces their aggressive behavior. Van Bockstaele and colleagues (2020) focused specifically on "hostile attribution bias modification training," for aggressive adolescents in the Netherlands. They created a five-session group intervention to train adolescents to make more benign interpretations of ambiguous provocations. Random assignment to the intervention reduced hostile attribution bias and decreased levels of reactive aggressive behavior. There was no effect on adolescents' proactive aggressive behavior.

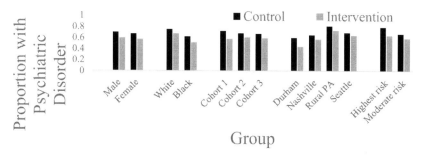

Figure 19 The impact of Fast Track on psychiatric disorder in adulthood, by subgroups (adapted from CPPRG, 2015).

Defensive mindset is one of the core constructs targeted in a broader set of interventions to improve children's social emotional learning (SEL). These interventions include classroom curricula designed to teach essential social-cognitive skills such as emotion recognition and social problem solving. Meta-analyses of the effectiveness of SEL interventions have repeatedly shown that curricular interventions are effective in improving these skills and have positive impact on children's social behavior that is sustained, sometimes, over many years (Cipriano et al., 2023). SEL interventions are particularly effective as universal approaches to reach the full population of children and can be effective as adjuncts to more comprehensive interventions for high-risk children, which is how the Fast Track program used the PATHS® curriculum.

6.2 What Has Been Learned from Fast Track

6.2.1 Young aggressive children are not necessarily destined to a life of violent crime.

A popular notion in the 1990s was that young aggressive behavior-problem children who disrupted their classrooms were "super-predators" (Bennett et al., 1996), who were genetically and biologically defective and should be segregated into special education classrooms, thrown out of school into "juvie" detention centers, and then imprisoned for long sentences as teenagers and adults (Bennett et al., 1996; Herrnstein & Murray, 1994). Intervention was thought to be futile, and society could be saved only by ridding these super-predators from schools and neighbor-hoods. It also happened that many of these children were African American. This idea was widespread in society and held by scholars and policy makers such as Herrnstein and Murray (1994). Standing in stark contrast, the Fast Track interven-tion challenges the notion of inevitable destiny, and the findings obtained through the randomized controlled trials show definitively that young aggressive children can be guided toward a trajectory of productive nonviolent adult lives.

6.2.2 The key psychological process that drives children to aggressive behavior is a defensive mindset, and the key to successful intervention is to address this mindset

If the large body of research summarized in this Element were not sufficient to drive home the idea that the key to understanding children's aggressive behavior is to understand defensive mindset, then the Fast Track intervention findings should close the case. A primary target of change in Fast Track was to help aggressive children view the world in a different way and from a different perspective than their defensive mindset. Even though these children may have come to be defensive as an understandable and adaptive response to a cruel world, the key to changing their life course would be to develop social-cognitive skills and reject perspectives that are captured in the notion of a defensive mindset. The evaluation of Fast Track shows this intervention can work: Aggressive children can learn these valuable skills and a new mindset. Furthermore, changing defensive mindset to a more open mindset is a key ingredient to the success of Fast Track.

6.2.3 Fast Track is not (yet) a viable model for at-scale implementation.

Fast Track achieved enduring positive change for aggressive children, and a cursory benefit–cost analysis shows the investment in Fast Track would likely yield a very favorable return on that investment. The Fast Track intervention cost about $58,000 per child over a ten-year period. According to Cohen (2005), the average life-persistent aggressive child grows up to cost society over $2,000,000 in judicial costs, incarceration, and cost to victims. Simple arithmetic shows a decrease in the prevalence of 2-million-dollar predators by just 3 percentage points would bring a positive rate of return on an investment of $58,000. Assume intervention with 100 children at $58,000 each, totaling $5.8 million. If just 3 of the 100 children were "saved" from otherwise becoming a 2-million-dollar predator, the savings would be $6 million, and the intervention would produce a positive return on investment. Of course, a more sophisticated analysis would bring in discounting due to inflation and other factors. The findings from the randomized trial show a much higher success rate from Fast Track: The rate of adult externalizing psychopathology was reduced by 10 percentage points, which is over 3 times the rate needed to break even. This is a 3-to-1 return on investment that would hold up to rigorous scrutiny.

So why is Fast Track not currently a viable model for scaling up to achieve population impact? Even with this success, the Fast Track intervention as implemented should not be scaled up in any large community for four reasons. First, the "success" achieved still left too many children growing up to have recurring problems. Although Fast Track reduced the rate of adult psychopathology in this high-risk group from 69% to 59%, that outcome still leaves too many children facing unsuccessful lives. An intervention would need to almost "wipe out" the problem (rather than modestly reduce it) for society to "buy" this approach. Second, the cost is too high. Even if the return is great, communities cannot, or will not, allocate such a large amount to "help" disruptive, aggressive children. The political will is not there, and the discretionary budget may not be there. Third, the intervention required a great deal of cooperation from teachers and school principals that is not likely to be forthcoming if the intervention is imposed on them. This problem became evident when children in Fast Track moved to new schools in remote districts. Principals at those schools could not be convinced to invest in school-wide curriculum changes for just one child who had been assigned to their school. Fourth, and perhaps most importantly, we learned that age 5 is relatively late to begin intervention for a process that starts earlier in life. We know the devastating impact of early adverse events. Intervention should start sooner.

6.2.4 To achieve greater success, the intervention needs to start early and reach universally.

The problems of chronically aggressive children are rooted in early threat and adversity, whether it is neglect due to poverty or trauma due to physical abuse or related exposures in the first five years of life. Threat leads to a defensive mindset. Once a pattern of defensive processing begins, it is self-reinforcing and becomes difficult to change. The problem needs to be attacked earlier in the life cycle, before abuse occurs and before neural pathways are established that cannot easily be "undone." Because early adverse events can occur in any sector of the population, the entire population of children and their families need to be reached in early life.

7 Defensive Mindset in Everyday Life

Despite Axelrod's assertion in 1981 that the long-term adaptiveness of reactive aggression is poor, many ecological contexts seem to encourage defensive processes such as hypervigilance, hostile attributions, and reactive aggression, at least for some members in some contexts. In the United States South, for example, a unique "culture of honor" (Nisbett, 1996) that began in colonial times has led citizens to display hypervigilance toward provocateurs, perceptual readiness to attribute hostile intent to others, and obligatory retaliatory aggression in response to being dishonored. Qualitative accounts of the "code of the street" in urban communities in the United States point toward the importance of retaliating against being "dissed," as in "disrespected" (Anderson, 1999). "Stand Your Ground" laws in the United States make it lawful to retaliate against another person if there is even only a slight indication that the other person might have threatened; it has become lawful to be biased in favor of assumed hostile attribution. The following domains are ripe for inspection of defensive mindset through more careful research and possible preventive intervention through culture change and public policy reform.

7.1 School Culture

Much of this Element is about children interacting in school settings. Education leaders may have few instruments to affect children's development, but they can implement policies that exacerbate or minimize children's defensive mindset.

School leaders have a large impact on students merely by the way they assign students to particular classrooms. The practice of tracking students by academic ability level (or special education status) has the effect of labeling students. The generally perceived overlap between low academic ability and high aggressive behavior problems may foment expectations by other students that low-tracked students are aggressive and should not be trusted. Peers may become hypervigilant toward tracked students. The low-tracked students may see their placement as a provocation, increasing their defensive mindsets. Tracking practices may need to be abolished or reformed.

School discipline policies can also affect students' mindsets. Policies and practices that place full blame and sanctions on a student without due process will only encourage students to develop a hostile world view. In contrast, policies such as positive behavioral interventions and supports (PBIS; Conradi et al., 2022) set positive expectations and require fair treatment of all students. These policies are likely to reduce defensive mindsets in students. They do not condone misbehavior, and they do not let students "get away with" misbehavior. Rather, they provide appropriate consequences and accountability for misbehavior while not allowing students to perpetuate a world view that all adults are threatening. PBIS policies support children's positive behavioral development (Conradi et al., 2022); these policies might have their impact through minimizing students' defensive mindset.

7.2 Parenting

Parenting practices can promote or mitigate development of children's defensive mindset. Parents themselves are subject to defensive mindset about their children. Parenting can be a lonely proposition. Especially for single parents and parents who come to have a baby without planning, an infant can be terribly disruptive, no matter how much a parent loves the baby. The baby is there 24/7. There is no relief. Resentment of the baby can grow. For new parents who have little experience and few on-site role models, a crying baby at 2 AM is an ambiguous provocation. Is the baby trying to keep me from sleeping? Does my baby hate me? Even middle-class parents in two-parent families can develop erroneous beliefs and hostile attributions about their baby.

I recall interviewing a well-educated, previously-employed mother whose husband was a fast-rising business executive. About six weeks after giving birth to her first baby, a baby that she did not plan or want to have, this woman found herself at home alone with the baby while her husband was enjoying himself on a business trip. In retrospect, the woman was clearly suffering from postpartum depression, although she was not in treatment. At 2 AM, the baby's ceaseless crying kept the mother awake. She was slow in responding. Finally, she got up out of her bed and went to the baby, who had a wet diaper. As she changed the diaper, he peed all over her face. In a fitful moment, she slapped her baby across the face, leaving a bruise that purpled by the morning. She took her baby to the pediatrician, who figured out what had happened and called Child Protective Services. When I interviewed her later, she said, with little emotion: "I was so tired. I think he knew it and was punishing me. He deserved it."

This woman apparently believed that six-week-old babies are capable of intentional actions (they are not), and furthermore, that her own baby had already grown to be mad at her.

Some mothers come to believe their baby can and will cause them harm. Berlin et al. (2013) administered a survey instrument to 500 mothers-to-be, in which they posed hypothetical situations in which their baby committed ambiguous provocations, such as peeing on them, crying incessantly, and refusing to take milk. The investigators asked the women to attribute intentions to the baby. Those pregnant women who showed a tendency to make hostile attributions about their infant-to-be were several times more likely than other women to show up on official registries for child abuse by infant age 24 months. Girod et al. (2023) also found that mothers' negative attributions about infant crying predicted lower sensitivity to their infant's distress.

Strassberg (1995) found that mothers of aggressive behavior problem boys demonstrated more hostile attributional biases in response to hypothetical situations in which they imagined their own child had misbehaved. When asked how and why their child might not comply, they used terms such as "defiant" rather than more benign explanations. Nix et al. (1999) similarly found that mothers who displayed hostile attributional biases and engaged in harsh discipline were relatively likely to have children who displayed similar patterns of behavior. The relations between hostile attributions and aggressive behavior cascade within families. Mothers' hostile attributional tendencies toward their children predict their harsh discipline practices with their children, which predict the children's hostile attributional biases (MacBrayer et al., 2003), which predict the children's development of aggressive behavior problems (Nix et al., 1999).

Because social support from others buffers a parent from developing wacky ideas about what an infant can do, parents should surround themselves with other parents and soak up as much knowledge as possible. The best way to become independently competent as a parent is to learn how to ask for help from others. Babies are babies: They are not trying to disrupt your life. Attend to their positive cues. Look for and savor every joyful moment.

7.3 Marriage

Romantic couples get into trouble in their marriage when they begin to view their partner as trying to be mean to them (Pourmohseni Koluri & Ranjbar, 2022).

> *"One partner ("Adrian") comes home from a long stressful day at work, tired, and ready to rest and relax. The other partner ("Chris") has been looking forward to their previously planned night out on the town and is ready to roll. Adrian does not understand why Chris is so uncaring and so cold at not recognizing Adrian's fatigue. Chris does not understand why Adrian is so uncaring and so cold at not recognizing Chris' enthusiasm about a big night out. Each has been hyper-vigilant to see signs the other is not being helpful and makes a hostile attribution about the other's intentions and behavior. Each feels a stream of emotions and lashes out in reactive anger, exasperation, and self-absorption. The marriage deteriorates."*

Skillful marital therapists can help with this problem by a version of the stop light. When tensions run high, slow things down (red light). Consider alternate interpretations of each other's actions and inquire rather than assume (yellow light). Negotiate and try out new solutions (green light). When things go wrong, start over (a new red light).

Well before a marital therapist is needed, couples can avoid going down this path by not making untested assumptions, giving each other the benefit of the doubt, keeping in focus the good reasons they got together in the first place, and making clear to the partner one's own good intentions so the partner will not go down the treacherous path.

7.4 The Workplace

The typical workplace is filled with bureaucratic policies, hierarchical relationships, competitive peer relationships, and enough stress to ignite conflicts based on misunderstandings. Policies about time off, paid sick leave, unscheduled required overtime, and vacation often are not explained well to frontline employees and often are interpreted by employees as maltreatment. This history of labor led to unionization. A long literature documents both the actual mistreatment and the perceptions of intentional mistreatment of employees (David et al., 2023). A similar literature documents the benefits of employee-friendly work policies, including employee voice in creating these policies, for employee satisfaction and ultimate company profit (Utah Women & Leadership Project, 2020).

Hierarchical (supervisor–supervisee) relationships, especially when boundaries are not made explicit, are prone to conflict due to misinterpretation and defensive mindset. A supervisee may have legitimate needs (e.g., an employee's daughter telephones with an emergency) that are misinterpreted by the supervisor as laggard behavior. A supervisor's attempts to befriend a supervisee to foster better working conditions may be misinterpreted as coercion or even sexual harassment. Of course, a long history of actual abuses makes occasional misinterpretations understandable. Although written policies may help prevent misinterpretation in some cases, respectful interpersonal practices embedded in the work culture and known policies for litigating conflicts are necessary to minimize problems.

Like family, neighborhood, and community contexts, the workplace is subject to problematic interpersonal conflicts among peers, particularly when competition for promotion and raises is present. These conflicts get exacerbated by stress. Policies that have been co-developed by employees and supervisors can mitigate workplace stress and reduce defensive mindset.

7.5 Race, Religion, Background, and Immigration

Contemporary society, heightened by the COVID pandemic and repeated trigger events such as the murder of George Floyd by police, is a hotbed of conflict across racial, ethnic, religious, and immigrant-status groups. Egregious and inexcusable disenfranchisement of persons of color grow defensive mindsets. The defensive mindset is the psychological process that potentiates much of cross-group conflict, and addressing this mindset could be a path toward improved relations.

7.6 Politics

Donald Trump is the prototype of defensive mindset gone haywire in politics. No matter what is said about him by a Democrat or mainstream media, he interprets the statement as a hostile, intentional slap in the face and presumes a self-righteous claim to retaliation. He must scour social media in a hypervigilant way to seek out possible insults against him. He over-interprets ambiguous, and even clearly benign, acts as threats to him. He reacts with emotional rage characterized by extreme psychophysiological arousal and loss of executive control. The only possible responses he contemplates are aggressive, and he sees these responses as justified and leading to favorable outcomes for himself. He places no value on good outcomes for others. Some observers might conclude his schtick is a planned strategy to rile up his base (whose members also play out a defensive mindset). Although his pattern may be so automatic by now that conscious self-awareness is not in play, the history of his development is surely a political case study.

The American political system fosters defensive mindset among its leaders and voters. Competitive elections require candidates to stake out positions that put themselves at odds with other candidates, rather than seeking common ground. Leaders' rhetoric stirs up voter support by focusing on negative statements about the other. Unfortunately, systematic research indicates negative statements about an opponent have greater impact than positive statements about oneself. The legislative system gives preference to political parties over issue-specific bilateral coalitions, and group identities foster cross-group stereotypes and defensive mindsets.

7.7 International Relations

An American airplane flies over Russian soil, and even though it is not clear whether the breach of air space was intentional, an international crisis ensues. Children throw rocks at military occupants in Northern Ireland, and war breaks out. This is the stuff of defensive mindset, played out among mistrusting nations.

I close with two anecdotes depicting sharply contrasting events in American history. Each is a tale of a President's possible defensive mindset, in the first case showing how a President's hostile attributional bias led the United States into war, and in the second case showing how a President's conscious attempt to avoid hostile attributional bias kept the world from mass destruction.

The first case is from 2003, following the tragedy of 9/11, when the United States feared terrorist attacks from everywhere. The attack on the United States led to communal post-traumatic stress and hypervigilance. The question was whether Iraqi President Saddam Hussein possessed weapons of mass destruction and posed a threat to US security. Although no one was sure, President George Bush ultimately made the decision to attack Iraq anyway. In an interview (King, 2002), he said, without proof,

"After all, this is the guy who tried to kill my dad" (George Bush, in King, 2002).

Over the next four years, an estimated 654,965 human beings died in the war in Iraq (Burnham et al., 2006). The war lasted more than a decade. It turned out that Iraq did not have nuclear weapons.

The second case is from October of 1962, when American spycraft determined the Soviet Union had placed loaded nuclear missiles in Cuba and pointed them toward the United States. Soviet Premier Nikita Khrushchev claimed American soldiers were occupying territory that bordered the Soviet Union. Hostile attributions abounded. The world expected a nuclear holocaust. Outside of public awareness, on October 26, 1962, US President John F. Kennedy received a cryptic message through an intermediary that the Soviets were willing to withdraw their missiles as long as the United States would agree not to invade the Soviet Union. It was a benignly intended act of peace.

Before Kennedy could breathe a sigh of relief and draft a written agreement to these terms, on the next morning of October 27, the President received a second message with a decidedly more hostile tone: The Soviet Union would launch nuclear missiles within the day unless the United States publicly backed down, acknowledged culpability, and withdrew its troops from Cuba and Turkey (May & Zelikow, 1997).

Audiotapes show that President Kennedy wanted to interpret Khrushchev's behavior benignly and wanted to demonstrate his own benign intentions. He could do so if he accepted the first message but not the second message. So what did he do? He decided to ignore the second message and to raise up the first message. He engineered his opponent's intention. On October 27, 1962, President Kennedy sent Soviet Premier Nikita Khrushchev the following note:

> "*I have read your letter of October 26 with great care and welcomed your statement of your desire to seek a prompt solution ... the United States is very much interested in reducing tensions ... I hope we can quickly agree ... (John F. Kennedy, in May & Zelikow, 1997).*"

And we are all still alive today.

References

Acland, E. L., Peplak, J., Suri, A., & Malti, T. (2023). Emotion recognition links to reactive and proactive aggression across childhood: A multi-study design. *Development and Psychopathology*, 1–12. https://doi.org/10.1017/S0954579423000342. Epub ahead of print. PMID: 37039136.

Aktas, V., Sahin, D., & Aydin, O. (2005). Hostile attributional bias in aggressive and nonaggressive children. *Turkish Journal of Psychology,. 20*(55), 43–59.

Anderson, E. (1989). *Code of the street: Decency, violence, and the moral life of the inner city.* New York: W.W. Norton.

Axelrod, R., & Hamilton, W. D. (1981). The evolution of cooperation. *Science, 211*(4489), 1390–1396. https://doi.org/10.1126/science.7466396.

Bandura, A. (1973). *Aggression: A social learning analysis.* Englewood Cliffs, NJ: Prentice-Hall.

Barefoot, J. C., Dahlstrom, W. G., & Williams, R. B. (1983). Hostility, CHD incidence, and total mortality: A 25-year follow-up study of 255 physicians. *Psychosomatic Medicine, 45*, 59–63.

Barefoot, J. C., Dodge, K. A., Peterson, B. L., Dahlstrom, W. G., & Williams, Jr., R. B. (1989). The Cook–Medley hostility scale: Item content and ability to predict survival. *Psychosomatic Medicine, 51*(1), 46–57. PMID: 2928460. https://doi.org/10.1097/00006842-198901000-00005.

Baron, R. M., & Kenny, D. A. (1986). The moderator–mediator variable distinction in social psychological research: Conceptual, strategic, and statistical considerations. *Journal of Personality and Social Psychology, 51*(6), 1173–1182. https://doi.org/10.1037/0022-3514.51.6.1173.

Bennett, W. J., Dilulio, J. J., & Walters, J. P. (1996). *Body count: Moral poverty and how to win America's war against crime and drugs.* New York: Simon and Schuster.

Belsky, J. (2014). Toward an evo-devo theory of reproductive strategy, health and longevity. *Perspectives in Psychological Science, 9*, 16–18.

Berkowitz, L. (Ed.). (1962). *Aggression: Social psychological analysis.* New York: McGraw-Hill.

Berlin, L. J., Appleyard, K., & Dodge, K. A. (2011). Intergenerational continuity in child maltreatment: Mediating mechanisms and implications for prevention. *Child Development, 82*(1), 162–176.

Berlin, L. J., Dodge, K. A., & Reznick, J. S. (2013). Examining pregnant women's hostile attributions about infants as a predictor of offspring maltreatment. *Journal American Medical Association Pediatrics*, *167*, 549–553. PMCID: PMC3753676. https://doi.org/10.1001/jamapediatrics .2013.1212.

Bierman, K. L., & Furman, W. (1984). The effects of social skills training and peer involvement on the social adjustment of preadolescents. *Child Development*, *55*(1), 151–162. https://doi.org/10.2307/1129841.

Bierman, K. L., Welsh, J. A., Hall, C. M., et al. (2022). Efficacy of the Fast Track friendship group program for peer-rejected children: A randomized-controlled trial. *Journal of Clinical Child and Adolescent Psychology*, *52*, 763–779. https:// doi.org/10.1080/15374416.2022.2051523.

Bookhout, M. K., Hubbard, J. A., Zajac, L., Mlawer, F. M., & Moore, C. C. (2021). Validation of the social information processing application (SIP-AP) across genders, socioeconomic levels, and forms of aggression. *Psychological Assessment*, *3*(8), 716–728. https://doi.org/10.1037/pas0001013.

Burks, V. S., Dodge, K. A., Price, J. M., & Laird, R. D. (1999). Internal representational models of peers: Implications for the development of problematic behavior. *Developmental Psychology*, *35*, 802–810.

Burks, V. S., Laird, R. D., Dodge, K. A., Pettit, G. S., & Bates, J. E. (1999). Knowledge structures, social information processing, and children's aggressive behavior. *Social Development*, *8*, 220–236. PMCID: PMC2792757.

Burnham, G., Lafta, R., Doocy, S., & Roberts, L. (2006). Mortality after the 2003 invasion of Iraq: A cross-sectional cluster sample survey. *The Lancet*. *368*(9545), 1421–1428. https://doi.org/10.1016/S0140-6736(06)69491-9. PMID 17055943. S2CID 23673934.

Caprara, G. V., Dodge, K. A., Pastorelli, C., & Zelli, A. (2007). How marginal deviations sometimes grow into serious aggression. *Child Development Perspectives*, *1*, 33–39. PMCID: PMC2747107.

Carré, J., Iselin, A-M., Welker, K., Hariri, A., & Dodge, K. A. (2014). Testosterone reactivity mediates the effect of early intervention on aggressive behavior. *Psychological Science*, *25*(5), 1140–1146. PMCID: PMC4278576. https://doi.org/10.1177/0956797614525642.

Cassidy, J., Kirsh, S. J., Scolton, K. L., & Parke, R. D. (1996). Attachment and representations of peer relationships. *Developmental Psychology*, *32*(5), 892–904. https://doi.org/10.1037/0012-1649.32.5.892.

Cipriano, C., Strambler, M. J., Naples, L. H., et al. (2023). The state of evidence for social and emotional learning: A contemporary meta-analysis of universal school-based SEL interventions. *Child Development*, *94*, 1181–1204. https:// doi.org/10.1111/cdev.13968.

Coe, J. L., Davies, P. T., Hentges, R. F., & Sturge-Apple, M. L. (2020). Detouring in the family system as an antecedent of children's adjustment problems.

Journal of Family Psychology, *34*(7), 814–824. https://doi.org/10.1037/fam0000727.

Cohen, M. A. (2005). *The costs of crime and justice*. New York: Routledge.

Coie, J. D., & Krehbiel, G. (1984). Effects of academic tutoring on the social status of low-achieving, socially rejected children. *Child Development*, *55*(4), 1465–1478. https://doi.org/10.2307/1130016.

Conduct Problems Prevention Research Group. (1999). Initial impact of the Fast Track Prevention Trial for Conduct Problems: I. The high-risk sample. *Journal of Consulting and Clinical Psychology*, *67*, 631–647. PMCID: PMC2762610.

Conduct Problems Prevention Research Group. (2002). Evaluation of the first three years of the Fast Track prevention trial with children at high risk for adolescent conduct problems. *Journal of Abnormal Child Psychology*, *30*(1), 19–35.

Conduct Problems Prevention Research Group. (2004). The effects of the Fast Track program on serious problem outcomes at the end of elementary school. *Journal of Clinical Child and Adolescent Psychology*, *33*, 650–661. PMCID: PMC2779517.

Conduct Problems Prevention Research Group. (2007). Fast Track randomized controlled trial to prevent externalizing psychiatric disorders: Findings from grades 3 to 9. *Journal of the American Academy of Child and Adolescent Psychiatry*, *46*, 1250–1262. PMCID: PMC2754206.

Conduct Problems Prevention Research Group. (2010). The difficulty of maintaining positive intervention effects: A look at disruptive behavior, deviant peer relations, and social skills during the middle school years. *Journal of Early Adolescence*, *30*, 593–624.

Conduct Problems Prevention Research Group. (2015). Impact of early intervention on psychopathology, crime, and well-being at age 25. *American Journal of Psychiatry*, *172*(1), 59–70. PMCID: PMC4485380. https://doi.org/10.1176/appi.ajp.2014.13060786.

Conduct Problems Prevention Research Group. (2019). *The Fast Track program for children at risk: Preventing antisocial behavior*. New York: Guilford Press.

Conradi, L. A., Walker, V. L., McDaid, P., Johnson, H. N., & Strickland-Cohen, M. K. (2022). A literature review of school-wide positive behavioral interventions and supports for students with extensive support needs (TIES Center Report 106). *TIES Center and the Center on PBIS*.

Crick, N. R., & Dodge, K. A. (1994). A review and reformulation of social information-processing mechanisms in children's social adjustment. *Psychological Bulletin*, *115*, 74–101.

Crick, N. R., & Dodge, K. A. (1996). Social-information-processing mechanisms in reactive and proactive aggression. *Child Development, 67*, 993–1002.

Crozier, J. C., Dodge, K. A., Fontaine, R. G., et al. (2008). Social information processing and cardiac predictors of adolescent antisocial behavior. *Journal of Abnormal Psychology, 117*, 253–267. PMCID: PMC3391970.

Curtis, W. J., & Cicchetti, D. (2011). Affective facial expression processing in young children who have experienced maltreatment during the first year of life: An event-related potential study. *Development and Psychopathology, 23*, 373–395.

David, E. M., Volpone, S. D., Avery, D. R., Johnson, L. U., & Crepeau, L. (2023). Am I next? Men and women's divergent justice perceptions following vicarious mistreatment. *Journal of Applied Psychology* (Online First Publication). https://doi.org/10.1037/apl0001109.

Dodge, K. A. (1976). *A randomized controlled trial of social role taking training with aggressive children.* Unpublished Master's Thesis. Durham, NC: Duke University .

Dodge, K. A. (1980). Social cognition and children's aggressive behavior. *Child Development, 51*(1), 162–170. PMID: 7363732.

Dodge, K. A. (1986). A social information processing model of social competence in children. In M. Perlmutter (Ed.), *Minnesota symposium in child psychology* (pp. 77–125). Hillsdale, NJ: Erlbaum.

Dodge, K. A. (2006). Translational science in action: Hostile attributional style and the development of aggressive behavior problems. *Development and Psychopathology, 18*, 791–814. PMCID: PMC2745254.

Dodge, K. A., & Newman, J. P. (1981). Biased decision-making processes in aggressive boys. *Journal of Abnormal Psychology, 90*(4), 375–379. PMID: https://doi.org/10.1037//0021-843x.90.4.375.

Dodge, K. A., & Frame, C. L. (1982). Social cognitive biases and deficits in aggressive boys. *Child Development, 53*(3), 620–635. PMID: 7094675.

Dodge, K. A., & Coie, J. D. (1987). Social information processing factors in reactive and proactive aggression in children's peer groups. *Journal of Personality and Social Psychology, 53*(6), 1146–1158. PMID: 3694454. https://doi.org/10.1037//0022-3514.53.6.1146.

Dodge, K. A., & Somberg, D. R. (1987). Hostile attributional biases among aggressive boys are exacerbated under conditions of threats to the self. *Child Development, 58*(1), 213–224. PMID: 3816345. https://10.1111/j.1467-8624 .1987.tb03501.x.

Dodge, K. A., & Tomlin, A. M. (1987). Utilization of self-schemas as a mechanism of interpretational bias in aggressive children. *Social Cognition, 5*(3), 280–300. https://doi.org/10.1521/soco.1987.5.3.280.

Dodge, K. A., & Price, J. M. (1994). On the relation between social information processing and socially competent behavior in early school-aged children. *Child Development, 65*(5), 1385–1398. PMID: 7982356. https://doi.org/10.1111/j.1467-8624.1994.tb00823.x.

Dodge, K. A., & Pettit, G. S. (2003). A biopsychosocial model of the development of chronic conduct problems in adolescence. *Developmental Psychology, 39*, 349–371. PMCID: PMC2755613.

Dodge, K. A., Murphy, R. R., & Buchsbaum, K. (1984). The assessment of intention-cue detection skills in children: Implications for developmental psychopathology. *Child Development, 55*(1), 163–173. PMID: 6705618.

Dodge, K. A., Godwin, J., & Conduct Problems Prevention Research Group. (2013). Social-information-processing patterns mediate the impact of preventive intervention on adolescent antisocial behavior. *Psychological Science, 24*(4), 456–465. PMCID: PMC3726052. https://doi.org/10.1177/0956797612457394.

Dodge, K. A., Malone, P. S., Lansford, J. E., et al. (2015). Hostile attributional bias and aggressive behavior in global context. *Proceedings of the National Academy of Sciences, 112*(30), 9310–9315. PMCID: PMC4522743. https://doi.org/10.1073/pnas.1418572112.

Dodge, K. A., Bai, Y., Godwin, J., et al (2022). A defensive mindset: A pattern of social information processing that develops early and predicts life course outcomes. *Child Development, 93*, e357–e378. https://doi.org/10.1111/cdev.13751.

Dodge, K. A., Pettit, G. S., McClaskey, C. L., & Brown, M. (1986). Social competence in children. *Monographs of the Society for Research in Child Development*, (Serial No. 213), *51*(2).

Dodge, K. A., Price, J. M., Bachorwski, J., & Newman, J. P. (1990). Hostile attributional biases in severely aggressive adolescents. *Journal of Abnormal Psychology, 99*(4), 385–392. PMID: 2266213. https://doi.org/10.1037//0021-843x.99.4.385.

Dodge, K. A., Pettit, G. S., Bates, J. E., & Valente, E. (1995). Social information-processing patterns partially mediate the effect of early physical abuse on later conduct problems. *Journal of Abnormal Psychology, 104*, 632–643.

Dodge, K. A., Lochman, J. E., Harnish, J. D., Bates, J. E., & Pettit, G. S. (1997). Reactive and proactive aggression in school children and psychiatrically impaired chronically assaultive youth. *Journal of Abnormal Psychology, 106*, 37–51.

Dodge, K. A., Laird, R., Lochman, J. E., Zelli, A., & Conduct Problems Prevention Research Group. (2002). Multidimensional latent-construct analysis of children's social information processing patterns: Correlations with aggressive behavior problems. *Psychological Assessment, 14*, 60–73.

Donovan, P. (2023). *Herbert Simon, Nobel 1978*. Do we understand human behavior? Online at: www.ubs.com/microsites/nobel-perspectives/en/laure ates/herbert-simon.html

Egan, S. K., Monson, T. C., & Perry, D. G. (1998). Social-cognitive influences on change in aggression over time. *Developmental Psychology, 34*(5), 996–1006. https://doi.org/10.1037/0012-1649.34.5.996

Feldman, E., & Dodge, K. A. (1987). Social information processing and sociometric status: Sex, age, and situational effects. *Journal of Abnormal Child Psychology, 15*(2), 211–227. PMID: 3611520. https://doi.org/10.1007/BF00916350

Fite, J. E., Bates, J. E., Holtzworth-Munroe, A., et al. (2008). Social information processing mediates the intergenerational transmission of aggressiveness in romantic relationships. *Journal of Family Psychology, 22*, 367–376. PMCID: PMC3396157.

Fontaine, R. G., & Dodge, K. A. (2006). Real-time decision making and aggressive behavior in youth: A heuristic model of response evaluation and decision (RED). *Aggressive Behavior, 32*, 604–624. PMCID: PMC2928648.

Fontaine, R. G., Burks, V. S., & Dodge, K. A. (2002). Response decision processes and externalizing behavior problems in adolescents. *Development and Psychopathology, 14*, 107–122.

Fontaine, R. G., Yang, C., Dodge, K. A., Bates, J. E., & Pettit, G. S. (2008). Testing an individual systems model of response evaluation and decision (RED) and antisocial behavior across adolescence. *Child Development, 79*, 462–475. PMCID: PMC3407957.

Forehand, R. L., & McMahon, R. J. (1981). *Helping the noncompliant child.* New York: Guilford.

Fraser, M. W., Galinsky, M. J., Smokowski, P. R., et al. (2005). Social information-processing skills training to promote social competence and prevent aggressive behavior in the third grade. *Journal of Consulting and Clinical Psychology, 73*(60), 1045–1055.

Garber, J., Quiggle, N. L., Panak, W., & Dodge, K. A. (1991). Aggression and depression in children: Comorbidity, specificity, and cognitive processing. In D. Cicchetti & S. Toth (Eds.), *Rochester symposium on developmental psychopathology, Vol. 2: Internalizing and externalizing expressions of dysfunction* (pp. 225–264). Hillsdale, NJ: Lawrence Erlbaum.

Girod, S. A., Leerkes, E. M., & Zvara, B. J. (2023). Childhood maltreatment predicts maternal sensitivity to distress: Negative attributions during the transition to parenthood. *Journal of Family Psychology, 37*(5),709–719. https://doi.org/10.1037/fam0001088. Epub April 13. PMID: 37053420; PMCID: PMC10440301.

Godwin, J., & Conduct Problems Prevention Research Group. (2020). The Fast Track intervention's impact on behaviors of despair in adolescence and young adulthood. *Proceedings of the National Academy of Sciences of the United States of America, 117*(5), 31748–31753. PMCID: PMC7749361. https://doi.org/10.1073/pnas.201623411.

Gouze, K. R. (1987). Attention and social problem solving as correlates of aggression in preschool males. *Journal of Abnormal Child Psychology, 15* (2), 181–197. https://doi.org/10.1007/BF00916348.

Graham, S., Hudley, C., & Williams, E. (1992). Attributional and emotional determinants of aggression among African-American and Latino young adolescents. *Developmental Psychology, 28*(4), 731–740. https://doi.org/10.1037/0012-1649.28.4.731.

Greenberg, M. T., & Kusche, C. A. (1993). *Promoting social and emotional development in deaf children: The PATHS project.* Seattle, WA: University of Washington Press.

Greenberg, M. T., Kusché, C. A., & Conduct Problems Prevention Research Group (2011). *Grade level PATHS (Grades 3–4).* South Deerfield, MA: Channing-Bete.

Hamlat, E. J., Prather, A. A., Horvath, S., Belsky, J., & Epel, E. S. (2021). Early life adversity, pubertal timing, and epigenetic age acceleration in adulthood. *Developmental Psychobiology, 63*, 890–902.

Herrnstein, R. J., & Murray, C. (1994). *The Bell Curve.* New York: Free Press.

Holbein, J. B. (2017). Childhood skill development and adult political participation. *American Political Science Review, 111*(3), 572–583. https://doi.org/10.1017/S0003055417000119.

Hosseini-Kamkar, N., Farahani, M. V., Nikolic, M., et al (2023). Adverse life experiences and brain function: A meta-analysis of functional magnetic resonance imaging findings. *JAMA Network Open, 6*(11), eE2340018. https://doi.org/10.1001/jamanetworkopen.2023.40018.

Hudley, C., & Graham, S. (1993). An attributional intervention to reduce peer-directed aggression among African-American boys. *Child Development, 64*(1), 124–138. PMID: 8436025.

Huesmann, L. R. (1988). An information processing model for the development of aggression. *Aggressive Behavior, 14*(1), 13–24. https://doi.org/10.1002/1098-2337(1988)14:1<13::AID-AB2480140104>3.0.CO;2-J

Huesmann, L. R., & Guerra, N. G. (1997). Children's normative beliefs about aggression and aggressive behavior. *Journal of Personality and Social Psychology*, *72*(2), 408–419. https://doi.org/10.1037/0022-3514.72.2.408

Jones, D., Godwin, J., Dodge, K. A., et al. (2010). Impact of the Fast Track prevention trial on health services use by conduct-problem youth. *Pediatrics*, *125*(1), 130–136. PMCID: PMC3534731. https://doi.org/10.1542/peds.2009-0322

Katsurada, E., & Sugawara, A. I. (1998). The relationship between hostile attributional bias and aggressive behavior in preschoolers. *Early Childhood Research Quarterly*, *13*(4), 623–636. https://doi.org/10.1016/S0885-2006(99)80064-7

Keil, V., & Price, J. M. (2009). Social information-processing patterns of maltreated children in two social domains. *Journal of Applied Developmental Psychology*, *30*(1), 43–52. https://doi.org/10.1016/j.appdev.2008.10.003

King, J. (2002). *Bush calls Saddam: "The guy who tried to kill my dad." CNN. com*. Posted 1:48am.

Kotlowitz, A. (1991). *There are no children here*. New York: Doubleday.

Lansford, J. E., & Dodge, K. A. (2008). Cultural norms for adult corporal punishment of children and societal rates of endorsement and use of violence. *Parenting: Science and Practice*, *8*, 257–270. PMCID: PMC2774244.

Lansford, J. E., Dodge, K. A., Pettit, G. S., et al. (2002). A 12-year prospective study of the long-term effects of early child physical maltreatment on psychological, behavioral, and academic problems in adolescence. *Archives of Pediatrics and Adolescent Medicine*, *156*, 824–830. PMCID: PMC2756659.

Lansford, J. E., Malone, P. S., Dodge, K. A., et al. (2006). A 12-year prospective study of patterns of social information processing problems and externalizing behaviors. *Journal of Abnormal Child Psychology*, *34*, 715–724. PMCID: PMC2753429.

Lansford, J. E., Miller-Johnson, S., Berlin, L. J., et al. (2007). Early physical abuse and later violent delinquency: A prospective longitudinal study. *Child Maltreatment*, *12*, 233–245. PMCID: PMC2771618.

Lansford, J. E., Malone, P. S., Dodge, K. A., et al. (2010). Children's perceptions of maternal hostility as a mediator of the link between discipline and children's adjustment in four countries. *International Journal of Behavioral Development*, *34*(5), 452–461. PMCID: PMC2930492. https://doi.org/10.1177/0165025409354933.

Lansford, J. E., Woodlief, D., Malone, P. S., et al. (2014). A longitudinal examination of mothers' and fathers' social information processing biases and harsh discipline in nine countries. *Development and Psychopathology, 26* (3), 561–573. PMCID: PMC4226066. https://doi.org/10.1017/S0954579 414000236.

Lansford, J. E., Godwin, J., Bornstein, M. H., et al. (2017). Reward sensitivity, impulse control, and social cognition as mediators of the link between childhood family adversity and externalizing behavior in eight countries. *Development and Psychopathology, 29*(5), 1675–1688. PMCID: PMC58 68955. https://doi.org/10.1017/S0954579417001328

Lansford, J. E., Godwin, J., McMahon R. J., et al. (2021). Early physical abuse and adult outcomes. *Pediatrics, 147*(1), e20200873. PMID: 33318226. https://doi.org/10.1542/peds.2020-0873

Lansford, J. E., Godwin, J., Dodge, K. A., et al. (2023). Fast Track intervention effects on family formation. *Journal of Family Psychology 37*(1), 54–64.

Lansford, J. E., Dodge, K. A., Pettit, G. S., & Bates, J. E. (2010). Does physical abuse in early childhood predict substance use in adolescence and early adulthood? *Child Maltreatment, 15*(2), 190–194. PMCID: PMC2868928. https://doi.org/10.1177/1077559509352359

Lansford, J. E., Malone, P. S., Dodge, K. A., Pettit, G. S., & Bates, J. E. (2010). Developmental cascades of peer rejection, social information processing biases, and aggression during middle school. *Development and Psychopathology, 22*(3), 593–602. PMCID: PMC2892817. https://doi.org/10.1017/S09545 79410000301

Lochman, J. E., & Dodge, K. A. (1994). Social-cognitive processes of severely violent, moderately aggressive, and nonaggressive boys. *Journal of Consulting and Clinical Psychology, 62*(2), 366–374. PMID: 8201075. https://doi.org/10.1037//0022-006x.62.2.366

MacBrayer, E. K., Milich, R., & Hundley, M. (2003). Attributional biases in aggressive children and their mothers. *Journal of Abnormal Psychology, 112*(4), 698–708.

MacKinnon-Lewis, C., Rabiner, D., & Starnes, R. (1999). Predicting boys' social acceptance and aggression: The role of mother–child interactions and boys' beliefs about peers. *Developmental Psychology, 35*(3), 632–639. https://doi.org/10.1037/0012-1649.35.3.632

May, E. R., & Zelikow, P. D. (Eds.). (1997). *The Kennedy tapes: Inside the White House during the Cuban missile crisis.* Cambridge, MA: Harvard University Press.

McCranie, E., Watkins, L., Brandsma, J., & Sisson, B. (1986). Hostility, CHD incidence, and total mortality: Lack of association in a 25-year follow-up study of 478 physicians. *Journal of Behavioral Medicine, 9,* 119–125.

McElwain, N. L., Booth-LaForce, C., Lansford, J. E., Wu, X., & Justin Dyer, W. (2008). A process model of attachment-friend linkages: Hostile attribution biases, language ability, and mother-child affective mutuality as intervening mechanisms. *Child Development, 79*(6), 1891–1906. https://doi.org/10.1111/j.1467-8624.2008.01232.x

Milich, R., & Dodge, K. A. (1984). Social information processing patterns in child psychiatric populations. *Journal of Abnormal Child Psychology, 12*(3), 471–490. PMID: 6747124. https://doi.org/10.1007/BF00910660

Murray, H. A. (1933). The effect of fear upon estimate of maliciousness of other personalities. *Journal of Social Psychology, 4*, 310–329.

Nisbett, R. (1996). *Culture of honor: The psychology of violence in the South.* New York: Westview Press.

Nix, R. L., Pinderhughes, E. E., Dodge, K. A., et al. (1999). The relation between mothers' hostile attribution tendencies and children's externalizing behavior problems: The mediating role of mothers' harsh discipline practices. *Child Development, 70*, 896–909.

Orbio de Castro, B., Veerman, J. W., Koops, W., Bosch, J. D., & Monsshouwer, H. J. (2002). Hostile attribution of intent and aggressive behavior: A meta-analysis. *Child Development, 73*(3), 916–934.

Patterson, G. R. (1976). The aggressive child: Victim and architect of a coercive system. In E. J. Mash, L. A. Hamerlynck, & L. C. Handy (Eds.), *Behavior modification and families* (pp. 267–316). New York: Brunner/Mazel.

Petersen, A. C., Joseph, J, & Feit, M. (Eds.). (2014). Consequences of child abuse and neglect. In *New Directions in Child Abuse and Neglect Research: Committee on Child Maltreatment Research, Policy, and Practice for the Next Decade: Phase II* (pp. 111–174). Board on Children, Youth, and Families; Committee on Law and Justice; Institute of Medicine; National Research Council. Washington, DC: National Academies Press.

Pettit, G. S., Bates, J. E., Dodge, K. A., & Meece, D. W. (1999). The impact of after-school peer contact on early adolescent externalizing problems is moderated by parental monitoring, neighborhood safety, and prior adjustment. *Child Development, 70*, 768–778. PMCID: PMC2761644.

Pettit, G. S., Lansford, J. E., Malone, P. S., Dodge, K. A., & Bates, J. E. (2010). Domain specificity in relationship history, social-information processing, and violent behavior in early adulthood. *Journal of Personality and Social Psychology, 98*(2), 190–200. PMCID: PMC3718014. https://doi.org/10.1037/a0017991

Pollak, S. D., & Kistler, D. J. (2002). Early experience is associated with the development of categorical representations for facial expressions of emotion. *Proceedings of the National Academy of Sciences, 99*(13), 9072–9076.

Pollak, S. D., Cicchetti, D., Klorman, R., & Brumaghim, J. T. (1997). Cognitive brain event-related potentials and emotion processing in maltreated children. *Child Development, 68,* 773–787.

Pollak, S. D., Messner, M., Kistler, D. J., & Cohn, J. F. (2009). Development of perceptual expertise in emotion recognition. *Cognition, 110,* 242–247.

Pollak, S. D. & Sinha, P. (2002). Effects of early experience on children's recognition of facial displays of emotion. *Developmental Psychology, 38,* 784–791.

Pourmohseni Koluri, F., & Ranjbar, H. (2022). The role of victim sensitivity, hostile attribution bias and anger rumination in predicting marital status. *Family Psychology, 8*(2), 73–85. https://doi.org/10.52547/ijfp.2022.536891.0

Quan, F., Yang, R., Zhu, W., et al. (2019). The relationship between hostile attribution bias and aggression and the mediating effect of rumination. *Personality and Individual Differences, 139*(1), 228–234.

Quiggle, N., Panak, W. F., Garber, J., & Dodge, K. A. (1992). Social information processing in aggressive and depressed children. *Child Development, 63* (6), 1305–1320. PMID: 1446554.

Ribordy S. C., Camras L. A., Stefani, R., & Spaccarelli, S. (1988). Vignettes for emotion recognition research and affective therapy with children. *Journal of Clinical Child Psychology, 17*(4), 322–325, DOI: 10.1207/s15374424jccp 1704_4

Rose, A. J., & Asher, S. R. (1999). Children's goals and strategies in response to conflicts within a friendship. *Developmental Psychology, 35*(1), 69–79. https://doi.org/10.1037/0012-1649.35.1.69

Rosen, H. J., & Levenson, R. W. (2009). The emotional brain: Combining insights from patients and basic science. *Neurocase: Behavior, Cognition, and Neuroscience, 15,* 173–181.

Schiele, B. C., Baker, A. B., & Hathaway, S. R. (1943). The Minnesota Multiphasic Personality Inventory. *Lancet,* (63), 292–297. ISSN 0096-0233.

Schwartz, D., McFadyen-Ketchum, S., Dodge, K. A., Pettit, G. S., & Bates, J. E. (1999). Early behavior problems as a predictor of later peer group victimization: Moderators and mediators in the pathways of social risk. *Journal of Abnormal Child Psychology, 27,* 191–201. PMCID: PMC 2761646.

Schwenck, C., Gensthaler, A., Romanos, M. et al. (2014). Emotion recognition in girls with conduct problems. *European Child and Adolescent Psychiatry,* 23, 13–22. https://doi.org/10.1007/s00787-013-0416-8

Shackman, J. E. & Pollak, S. D. (2005). Experiential influences on multimodal perception of emotion. *Child Development, 76,* 1116–1126.

Shekelle, R., Gale, M., Ostfeld, A., & Paul, O. (1983). Hostility, risk of coronary heart disease, and mortality. *Psychosomatic Medicine, 45*, 109–114.

Selman, R. L. (1976). The development of social-cognitive understanding: A guide to educational and clinical practice. In T. Licona (Ed.), *Morality: Theory, research, and social issues* (pp. 299–316). New York: Holt, Reinhart and Winston.

Simon, H. A. (1967). Motivational and emotional controls of cognition. *Psychological Review, 74*(1), 29–39. https://doi.org/10.1037/h0024127

Sinclair, A. H., Wang, Y. C., & Adcock, A. (2023). Instructed motivational states bias reinforcement learning and memory formation. *Proceedings of the National Academy of Sciences, 20*(31), 1–12. https://doi.org/10.1073/pnas.2304881120

Smithmyer, C. M., Hubbard, J. A., & Simons, R. F. (2000). Proactive and reactive aggression in delinquent adolescents: Relations to aggression outcome expectancies. *Journal of Clinical Child Psychology, 29*(1), 86–93. https://doi.org/10.1207/S15374424jccp2901_9

Sorensen, L. C., Dodge, K. A., & Conduct Problems Prevention Research Group. (2016). How do childhood interventions prevent crime? *Child Development, 87*(2), 429–445.

Steinberg, M. D., & Dodge, K. A. (1983). Attributional bias in aggressive adolescent boys and girls. *Journal of Social and Clinical Psychology, 1*(4), 312–321. https://doi.org/10.1521/jscp.1983.1.4.312

Steinberg, L., Icenogle, G., Shulman, E., et al. (2018). Around the world, adolescence is a time of heightened sensation seeking and immature self-regulation. *Developmental Science, 21*, 1–13.

Strassberg, Z. (1995). Social information processing in compliance situations by mothers of behavior-problem boys. *Child Development, 66*, 376–383.

Tuente, S. K., Bogaerts, S., & Veling, W. (2019). Hostile attribution bias and aggression in adults – A systematic review. *Aggression and Violent Behavior, 46*, 66–81.

Tottenham, N., Tanaka, J. W., Leon, A. C., et al. (2009). The NimStim set of facial expressions: Judgments from untrained research participants. *Psychiatry Research, 168*(3), 242–249.

Utah Women & Leadership Project (2020). Flexible and-friendly policies at Utah's best places to work. *Research & Policy Brief, 27*.

Van Bockstaele, B., van der Molen, M. J., van Niewenhuijzen, M., & Salemink, E. (2020). Modification of hostile attribution bias reduces self-reported reactive aggressive behavior in adolescents. *Journal of Experimental Child Psychology, 194*(6), 104811. https://doi.org/10.1016/j.jecp.2020.104811

Verhoef, R. E. J., Alsem, S. C., Verhulp, E. E., & O. De Castro, B. (2019). Hostile intent attribution and aggressive behavior in children revisited: A meta-analysis. *Child Development, 90*(5), e525–e547. https://doi.org/10.1111/cdev.13255.

Walters, G. D. (2007). Measuring proactive and reactive criminal thinking with the PICTS: Correlations with outcome expectancies and hostile attribution biases. *Journal of Interpersonal Violence, 22*(4), 371–385. https://doi.org/10.1177/0886260506296988

Weiss, B., Dodge, K. A., Bates, J. E., & Pettit, G. S. (1992). Some consequences of early harsh discipline: Child aggression and a maladaptive social information processing style. *Child Development, 63*(6), 1321–1335. PMID: 1446555. https://doi.org/10.1111/j.1467-624.1992.tb01697.x

Weissberg, R. P., Caplan, M., Bennetto, L., & Jackson, A. S. (1990). *The New Haven Social Development Program: Sixth grade social problem-solving module.* Chicago, IL: University of Illinois at Chicago.

Yaros, A., Lochman, J. E., & Wells, K. (2016). Parental aggression as a predictor of boys' hostile attribution across the transition to middle school. *International Journal of Behavioral Development, 40*(5), 452–458. https://doi.org/10.1177/0165025415607085

Yechiam, E., Goodnight, J., Bates, J. E., et al. (2006). A formal cognitive model of the Go/No-Go discrimination task: Evaluation and implications. *Psychological Assessment, 18*, 239–249. PMCID: PMC2752340.

Yoo, G., & Park, J. H. (2019). Influence of hostile attribution bias on cyberbullying perpetration in middle school students and the multiple additive moderation effect of justice sensitivity. *Koran Journal of Child Studies, 40*(4), 79–93.

Zajac, L., Bookhout, M. K., Hubbard, J. A., Carlson, E. A., & Dozier, M. (2020). Attachment disorganization in infancy: A developmental precursor to maladaptive social information processing at age 8. *Child Development, 91*(1), 145–162. https://doi.org/10.1111/cdev.13140

Zelli, A., Dodge, K. A., Lochman, J. E., Laird, R. D., & Conduct Problems Prevention Research Group. (1999). The distinction between beliefs legitimizing aggression and deviant processing of social cues: Testing measurement validity and the hypothesis that biased processing mediates the effects of beliefs on aggression. *Journal of Personality and Social Psychology, 77*, 150–166.

Acknowledgments

Growing up on the South Side of Chicago during the 1950s and 1960s exposed me to violence in many forms. I thank my mother and father for protecting me and instilling in me a sense of responsibility to make the world a safer place. As a child, I thought I could contribute by becoming a juvenile court judge, but my academic mentors helped me realize that more lasting change could come from scientific discovery. I am grateful to my dissertation advisor, John Coie, for his generosity and friendship. All worthy scientific ideas are borne in interpersonal discourse and owned by a community, and I have been fortunate to work in remarkable intellectual communities at Indiana University, Vanderbilt University, and Duke University, with colleagues Richard McFall, Judy Garber, and Steven Hollon. For the ideas in this volume, I am grateful to many collaborators, particularly Jack Bates and Greg Pettit in the Child Development Project; Joseph Price and Virginia Burks in the Social Development Project; Jennifer Lansford, Jennifer Godwin, Ann Skinner, and the cast of the PAC Project; and Karen Bierman, Max Crowley, John Coie, Mark Greenberg, John Lochman, Robert McMahon, and Ellen Pinderhughes in Fast Track. I thank Marc Bornstein as Editor of this Cambridge Elements series and several anonymous reviewers. Over the past 45 years, I have worked with literally hundreds of talented undergraduate and graduate students, research assistants, and postdoctoral fellows. Thank you. Most importantly, I am grateful for the love and gifts from my wife, Claudia Jones, M.D., and my children, Graham and Zoë.

Cambridge Elements ᐦ

Child Development

Marc H. Bornstein
National Institute of Child Health and Human Development,
Bethesda Institute for Fiscal Studies,
London UNICEF, New York City

Marc H. Bornstein is an Affiliate of the Eunice Kennedy Shriver National Institute of Child Health and Human Development, an International Research Fellow at the Institute for Fiscal Studies (London), and UNICEF Senior Advisor for Research for ECD Parenting Programmes. Bornstein is President Emeritus of the Society for Research in Child Development, Editor Emeritus of *Child Development*, and founding Editor of *Parenting: Science and Practice.*

About the Series
Child development is a lively and engaging, yet serious and real-world subject of scientific study that encompasses myriad theories, methods, substantive areas, and applied concerns. Cambridge Elements in Child Development addresses many contemporary topics in child development with unique, comprehensive, and state-of-the-art treatments of principal issues, primary currents of thinking, original perspectives, and empirical contributions to understanding early human development.

Cambridge Elements ≡

Child Development

Elements in the Series

A full series listing is available at: www.cambridge.org/EICD

Printed in the United States
by Baker & Taylor Publisher Services